THE WORD OF THE CROSS

THE WORD OF THE CROSS

MARTIN LUTHER'S HEIDELBERG DISPUTATION

CHARLES FRY

The Word of the Cross: Martin Luther's Heidelberg Disputation

Published by:
1517 Publishing
PO Box 54032
Irvine, CA 92619-4032

Cover design by Brenton Clarke Little.

Printed in the United States of America

Publisher's Cataloging-In-Publication Data
(Prepared by The Donohue Group, Inc.)

Names: Fry, Charles (Charles Edward), 1962-
Title: The word of the Cross : Martin Luther's Heidelberg disputation / Charles Fry.
Description: Irvine, CA : 1517 Publishing, [2018] | Originally presented as the author's thesis (M.A.)—Concordia University Irvine, 2017. | Includes bibliographical references.
Identifiers: ISBN 9781945978173 (softcover) | ISBN 9781945978180 (ebook)
Subjects: LCSH: Luther, Martin, 1483–1546. Disputatio Heidelbergae habita. | Luther, Martin, 1483–1546—Criticism and interpretation. | Religious disputations—Germany. | Jesus Christ—Crucifixion. | Theology of the cross.
Classification: LCC BR332.5 .F79 2018 (print) | LCC BR332.5 (ebook) | DDC 230/.41/092—dc23

1517 Publishing, an imprint of 1517. The Legacy Project, is committed to packaging and promoting the finest content for fueling a new Lutheran Reformation. We promote the defense of the Christian faith, confessional Lutheran theology, vocation and civil courage.

To
C. FitzSimons and Martha Allison—
my very dear friends

Contents

"For the word of the cross is to those who are perishing foolishness, but to us who are being saved it is the power of God. For it is written,

> 'I WILL DESTROY THE WISDOM OF THE WISE,
> AND THE CLEVERNESS OF THE CLEVER I WILL SET ASIDE.'

Where is the wise man? Where is the scribe? Where is the debater of this age? Has not God made foolish the wisdom of the world? For since in the wisdom of God the world through its wisdom did not come to know God, God was well-pleased through the foolishness of the message preached to save those who believe."

1 Corinthians 1:18–21

Acknowledgments

It is with great joy that I express thanks to the following people: I wish to thank my advisor, Dr. Scott Keith, for being such an encourager as I worked on this book. To my professors at Christ College, Concordia University Irvine, I am thankful for their simplicity and faithfulness to the doctrine of *Solus Christus*. I am also grateful to New Reformation Press and their interest in this book. Working with them has been a great delight. I also wish to thank my brothers and sisters in Christ in Huntington who are such faithful and loving friends. I am thankful for their love for our family and their trust in "the word of the cross," Jesus Christ and Him crucified. Gratitude also goes to Brad Willis for his kindness in proofreading the book.

To my family: Thank you, Mom and Dad, for your faithful love for me. Thank you as well for the example of your quiet faithfulness to one another in a world that has said farewell to transcendent truth. Thank you, Lisa, "my rib." You are a beautiful theologian of the cross who smiles at the future (Prov. 31:25). Thank you, dear Heidi, for being our happy little daughter who skips when everyone else merely walks. May you ever rest in the unchanging love and grace of Christ all the days of your life, no matter what may come.

Abbreviations

AE	*Luther's Works (American Edition)*
AUG	*On the Spirit and the Letter*
GREEN	*How Melanchthon Helped Luther Discover the Gospel*
HD	*The Heidelberg Disputation*
LTCF	*Luther's Theology of the Cross Fifteen Years after Heidelberg: Lectures on the Psalms of Ascent*
NIC	*Nicomachean Ethics*
OX	*Oxford Handbook of Martin Luther's Theology*
PT	*The Philosophical Theses and Demonstrations of the Heidelberg Disputation*
TOCL	*Luther's Theology of the Cross* (Loewenich)
TOCM	*Luther's Theology of the Cross* (McGrath)
RR	*The Annotated Luther, Volume 1: The Roots of Reform*
VERC	*Luther's Theology of the Cross at the Time of the Heidelberg Disputation*
WA	*D. Martin Luthers Werke* 1 (Weimar)

Preface

In the spring of 1518, Martin Luther was asked by Johann von Staupitz to give a disputation to the Augustinian monks at Heidelberg. Seeking to disentangle the Christian message from Aristotle and scholastic theology, he presented forty theses that presented the true Christian message stripped of medieval trappings. Given only a few months after Luther presented the *Ninety-Five Theses*, the Heidelberg Disputation has often been overshadowed by the events of the previous October. Yet the disputation would ultimately prove to be an outline of the Protestant message and of Luther's "subsequent theological program."[1]

The message of the Heidelberg Disputation is that God is not known by human wisdom, but He is revealed in suffering and the cross. It is God's message, which the world in its hubristic wisdom considers to be foolishness. The goal of this book is to unfold what Luther taught at Heidelberg and why it was so important to him—and to us. The ramifications of his argument have everything to do with the course of human history, the welfare of Christ's Church, and the trajectory and comfort of our own lives as well.

More than once have I been humbled in writing this book. First, my inadequacy has been acutely felt as I encountered the capacious academic work of Luther scholars. I owe an inexpressible debt to these men for plowing up hard ground so that I may be helped in my study of the disputation and the writing of this book.

---

[1] Gerhard O. Forde, *On Being a Theologian of the Cross: Reflections on Luther's Heidelberg Disputation, 1518* (Grand Rapids: Eerdmans, 1997), 21.

However, much more than the work of Luther scholars, I have been left speechless and in awe by the very truth of what Luther presented in April 1518. In short, Luther's message (which is really God's message as described in First Corinthians 1) is like a scythe in the hands of the Lord laying flat the souls of the entire world before Him. No other message in history has had such a powerful effect as has God's "foolish" and "weak" message. It exposes the truth about each of us—not to leave us in despair (as the disputation itself asserts), but to bring us to genuine hope and joy found in the promise of Christ and His finished work on the cross. It enables one to become a theologian of the cross who "calls a thing what it actually is," telling the truth about God, ourselves, and the freeness and splendor of His grace in Christ. Luther's Heidelberg Disputation exposes the presuppositions of ideologies for what they really are: bankrupt systems of belief that will ultimately crumble before the splendor of the majesty of God (Isa. 2:11, 17). The disputation becomes a standard by which to evaluate all religions and the philosophies of all civilizations, leaving us with Christ and His cross as our only boast and true and permanent foundation.

April 2018 marks the five-hundredth anniversary of the Heidelberg Disputation. Therefore, this is a fitting time to revisit this wonderful work with the hope that God's Spirit may apply it to our lives in the twenty-first century. In the introduction to *Luther's Theology of the Cross*, Alister McGrath wrote the following: "It must never be forgotten that the theology of the cross is far more than an historical idea. The increasing recognition of the shallowness and naïveté of much Christian thinking about God and man has caused many to begin to retrace the steps taken by Luther before them, and to join him as he kneels at the foot of the cross, and adores the God who is 'hidden in suffering.' If the present study assists to increase that number, it will more than have served its purpose."[2]

This book shares McGrath's hope—for the honor of God and for the comfort and everlasting joy of His people.

---

[2] TOCM, 2, 3.

The Text of the Heidelberg Disputation[1]

Brother Martin Luther, Master of Sacred Theology, will preside and Brother Leonhard Beier, Master of Arts and Philosophy, will defend the following theses before the Augustinians of this renowned city of Heidelberg in the customary place. In the month of May, 1518.

Distrusting completely our own wisdom, according to that counsel of the Holy Spirit, "Do not rely on your own insight" (Prov. 3:5), we humbly present to the judgment of all those who wish to be here these theological paradoxes so that it may become clear whether they have been deduced well or poorly from St. Paul, the especially chosen vessel and instrument of Christ, and also from St. Augustine, his most trustworthy interpreter.

Theological Theses

1. The law of God, the most salutary doctrine of life, cannot advance man on his way to righteousness, but rather hinders him.
2. Much less can human works, which are done over and over again with the aid of natural precepts, so to speak, lead to that end.
3. Although the works of man always appear attractive and good, they are nevertheless likely to be mortal sins.
4. Although the works of God always seem unattractive and appear evil, they are nevertheless really eternal merits.

[1] From RR, 80–88.

5. The works of men are thus not mortal sins (we speak of works which are apparently good), as though they were crimes.
6. The works of God (we speak of those which he does through man) are thus not merits, as though they were sinless.
7. The works of the righteous would be mortal sins if they would not be feared as mortal sins by the righteous themselves out of pious fear of God.
8. By so much more are the works of man mortal sins when they are done without fear and in unadulterated, evil self-security.
9. To say that works without Christ are dead, but not mortal, appears to constitute a perilous surrender of the fear of God.
10. Indeed, it is very difficult to see how a work can be dead and at the same time not a harmful and mortal sin.
11. Arrogance cannot be avoided or true hope be present unless the judgment of condemnation is feared in every work.
12. In the sight of God sins are then truly venial when they are feared by men to be mortal.
13. Free will, after the fall, exists in name only, and as long as it does what it is able to do, it commits a mortal sin.
14. Free will, after the fall, has power to do good only in a passive capacity, but it can do evil in an evil capacity.
15. Nor could the free will endure in a state of innocence, much less do good, in an active capacity, but only in a passive capacity.
16. The person who believes that he can obtain grace by doing what is in him adds sin to sin so that he becomes doubly guilty.
17. Nor does speaking in this manner give cause for despair, but for arousing the desire to humble oneself and seek the grace of Christ.
18. It is certain that man must utterly despair of his own ability before he is prepared to receive the grace of Christ.

19. That person does not deserve to be called a theologian who looks upon the invisible things of God as though they were clearly perceptible in those things which have actually happened (Rom. 1:20).
20. He deserves to be called a theologian, however, who comprehends the visible and manifest things of God seen through suffering and the cross.
21. A theologian of glory calls evil good and good evil. A theologian of the cross calls the things what it actually is.
22. That wisdom which sees the invisible things of God in works as perceived by man is completely puffed up, blinded and hardened.
23. The law brings the wrath of God, kills, reviles, accuses, judges, and condemns everything that is not in Christ (Rom. 4:15).
24. Yet that wisdom is not of itself evil, nor is the law to be evaded; but without the theology of the cross man misuses the best in the worst manner.
25. He is not righteous who does much, but he who, without work, believes much in Christ.
26. The law says, "Do this" and it is never done. Grace says, "Believe in this" and everything is already done.
27. Actually one should call the work of Christ an acting work and our work an accomplished work, and thus an accomplished work pleasing to God by the grace of the acting work.
28. The love of God does not find, but creates, that which is pleasing to it. The love of man comes into being through that which is pleasing to it.

Philosophical Theses

29. Whoever wishes without danger to philosophize using Aristotle must beforehand become thoroughly foolish in Christ.
30. Just as no one uses the evil of lust properly unless married, so nobody philosophizes well unless a fool—that is, a Christian.

31. It was easy for Aristotle to believe that the world was eternal since he believed that the human soul was mortal.
32. After it was held (by Aristotle) that there are just as many substantial forms as composite ones, it was necessary to hold that there are just as many material ones.
33. Nothing comes about necessarily from any particular reality in the world; nevertheless, necessarily whatever comes about naturally, comes about from matter.
34. If Aristotle recognized "the absolute power of God," he would have maintained that it is impossible for matter to exist unformed (*nudam*).
35. According to Aristotle, there is no actual infinite, yet with respect to potentiality and form there are as many infinities as there are composite things.
36. Aristotle wrongly rebukes and lampoons the philosophy of "Platonic ideas," a philosophy that is better than his own.
37. The "imitation of numbers" in things is cleverly asserted by Pythagoras, but cleverer still is the participation of ideas asserted by Plato.
38. The disputation of Aristotle (if a Christian will pardon this) "fights against" Parmenides' idea of oneness "by beating the air" (1 Cor. 9:26).
39. If Anaxagoras posited the infinite before form (of things), as it seems he did, he was the best of the philosophers, even if Aristotle was unwilling to acknowledge this.
40. To Aristotle, privation, matter, form, mobility, immobility, actuality, potentiality, etc. seem to be the same thing.

Numina cœleſtem nobis peperere Lutherum,
Noſtra diu maius ſæcla videre nihil.
Quem ſi Pontificum crudelis deprimit error,
Non feret iratos impia terra Deos.

This woodcut (c. 1520) is by the artist Hans Baldung Grien (1484–1545). Luther is here depicted as an Augustinian monk—much as he would have appeared at Heidelberg in 1518.

Courtesy of the Richard C. Kessler Reformation Collection, Pitts Theology Library, Candler School of Theology, Emory University.

Drawing of Heidelberg from 1572.
Courtesy of Wikimedia.

1

Introduction

On the Way to Corinth

"How a revolution erupts from a commonplace event—tidal wave from a ripple—is cause for endless astonishment."[1] So wrote the historian Jacques Barzun as he reflected on the Reformation and western culture's last five hundred years. The "tidal wave" that happened in the sixteenth century was the tearing apart of Europe and the Church that undergirded European society.[2] The "ripple" was a relatively obscure monk from Saxon Germany who wanted a calm conscience before the holiness of God's Law.[3]

---

[1] Jacques Barzun, *From Dawn to Decadence: 500 Years of Western Cultural Life* (New York: HarperCollins, 2000), 7.

[2] "If you study the sixteenth century, you are inevitably present at something like the aftermath of a particularly disastrous car crash. All around are half demolished structures, debris, people figuring out how to make sense of their lives that have suddenly been transformed." Diarmaid MacCulloch, *All Things Made New: The Reformation and Its Legacy* (Oxford: Oxford University Press, 2016), 1.

[3] "So the Reformation was not caused by social and economic forces, or even by a secular idea like nationalism; it sprang from a big idea about death, salvation and the afterlife . . . nothing that human beings could do, nothing of the intricate structure of intercessory prayer for the dead . . . could alter His decision, born of His own mercy and judgement. That is the thought that seized the German friar Martin Luther (1483–1546) and inspired so many people in Europe, and that is what brought this immense and powerful structure down." Ibid., 3.

Sixteenth-century Europe was a beehive of spiritual activity, energized by the Church's belief that human nature was spiritually *sick* yet able to heal itself. The old Church believed that all people were guilty before God but that by cooperating with an elaborate religious system of works, man could be healed and ultimately stand justified before the majesty of God's bar. By 1518, this religious system had become a religion of merit, a synthesis of Aristotle and the Bible, and a placing of reason and revelation on equal terms. The name given to this synthesis was *scholastic theology*. By cooperating with God's grace and by carefully running through the gauntlet of scholasticism's subtle theological system, one could shorten time in purgatory on the way to paradise. Gabriel Biel's (c. 1420–1495) dictum seemed to be ubiquitous: God will not deny His grace to one who does all that is within him. "In accordance with God's gracious goodness (*ex liberalitate*), he who does his best in a state of nature receives grace as a fitting reward (*meritum de congruo*)."[4]

Because of belief that human nature is sick but able to be healed, the Roman Church that dominated European society clung to the centrality of the Mass, purgatory, indulgences, the penitential system, relics, and a host of other means to appropriate God's help. God's grace was the medicine that enabled one to become attractive in His sight; human works of condignity and congruity were the means by which the medicine of His grace was appropriated. Such "loveliness," then, made one acceptable to God. Therefore, as Euan Cameron observed with a subtle understatement, "traditional Europe was a busy place."[5]

If the sixteenth-century Western church declared human nature to be merely sick, Martin Luther (1483–1546) declared the human heart to be spiritually *dead,* unable to will or to contribute one spark toward salvation. Humans were entirely dependent on the free and sovereign grace of God—a work that had its source entirely outside of a person, found only in the person and work of Christ. Aristotelian

---

[4] Steven Ozment, *The Age of Reform 1250–1550: An Intellectual and Religious History of Late Medieval and Reformation Europe* (New Haven: Yale University Press, 1980), 234.

[5] Euan Cameron, *The European Reformation* (Oxford: Oxford University Press, 2013), 18.

scholasticism was for Luther an illusion, a speculative sham. No human reason or works of the Law could be rendered to make man worthy in God's sight—even works done with God's help. God simply could not be known by human reason, wisdom, or merit. Man's will itself was not free, Luther declared. Comparing Luther to Augustine, Diarmaid MacCulloch wrote, "Augustine called a human being such as himself 'a lump of perdition'—a lump of lostness."[6] This concern to see the Church shorn of its misguided confidence in human reason and human works was lodged in Luther's heart when, on April 11, 1518,[7] he left Wittenberg, Germany, to give a disputation to a group of Augustinian monks in Heidelberg.

What is the message of the Heidelberg Disputation, and how did this message differ from the medieval church's theology? The message of the Heidelberg Disputation is summarized as follows: God is not known by human wisdom, but He is revealed through suffering and the cross. God is not known by human wisdom—that is, by the belief that man can somehow reach God by rendering good works to Him and by a belief that is based on man's reason or opinion. However, He is revealed through suffering and the cross—that is, as God humbles the sinner and brings a person to the end of human effort, He brings him or her to come to truly know Him by pure grace. And God can only be known in Christ—specifically, Christ crucified.

The Heidelberg Disputation was presented in forty theses on April 26[8] by Luther's colleague, Leonhard Beier. The first twenty-eight were theological and the last twelve were philosophical, intended to address what Luther saw as the foundational error in

---

[6] MacCulloch, *All Things Made New*, 4.

[7] Scott H. Hendrix, *Martin Luther: Visionary Reformer* (New Haven: Yale University Press, 2015), 68. Martin Brecht pinpoints Luther as leaving "after 9 April," yet also notes that Luther "decided to travel on foot" on March 21. Martin Brecht, *Martin Luther: His Road to Reformation 1483–1521* (Philadelphia: Fortress Press, 1985), 213, 214.

[8] Brecht asserts the HD took place in one day at the liberal arts faculty lecture hall at the university. Ibid., 215. Hendrix says the disputation took place on the April 26 and the 27, the first day at the Augustinian monastery, the second day at the lecture hall at the university. Hendrix, *Visionary Reformer*, 70.

scholasticism. The disputation's theology would continue to be developed in Luther's thought and eventually be reflected in the outline of all Protestant theology. Remarkably, this theology would also eventually tear Europe apart.

Three key observations—three subthemes—emerge from this study of the Heidelberg Disputation. First, in 1518, Luther was still developing in his understanding of the gospel; therefore, the Heidelberg Disputation was a transitional work. While his "evangelical breakthrough" had already begun by the time he arrived in Heidelberg, Luther was still "focusing the lens" of his understanding of justification. Second, while in 1518 Luther could not have known his future or the future of western Christianity, the Heidelberg Disputation became a paradigmatic outline of what would later be known as Protestant theology. It is an embryonic representation of the theology that would shape and undergird his remaining life and the future of Protestantism. The third observation is perhaps the most important of the three. In the Heidelberg Disputation, Luther made the claim that human nature is spiritually dead and therefore God cannot be known or approached by anything or any good in us. Salvation is entirely outside of us, found in Christ alone. If this is true, then not only was the entire scaffolding of medieval religion a rusted shamble; every civilization or culture that had built on the belief that human nature is good had built with a presuppositional lie—a rusted shamble. The Heidelberg Disputation gives us a baseline by which we may evaluate all cultures, all ideology, all theologies, and all history.

Chapter 1 presents the flow of the argument of this book as well as a brief review of scholarship that has been done on the disputation. The chapter ends with a study of Luther's "baseline" for the Heidelberg Disputation: the apostle Paul's message of the cross as found in 1 Corinthians 1:18–31, which describes the strangeness of the message of the cross and the unlikely people whom God chooses by this message.[9] Chapter 2 examines the context of the disputation in the areas of Aristotelian philosophy, scholasticism, mysticism,

[9] "Against this background Luther's use of the phrase and development of the idea of a 'theology of the cross' took shape on the basis of 1 Corinthians i.18–ii.16." Robert Kolb, LTCF, 71.

and Augustine's theology. Luther's personal life up to 1518 is also considered. On his way to Heidelberg, Luther had clearly given much thought to these issues and how to untangle the apostle Paul's message of the cross from the errors of medieval theology and its ensuing scholastic religion of merit.

The third chapter seeks to give exposition to the forty theses in light of the medieval and Renaissance context in which he lived. This exposition shows how the disputation stripped scholastic theology and the religion of his day of all human effort and pride, leaving only Christ. In doing so, Luther echoed Paul's argument in 1 Corinthians 1 and defended the power and wisdom of God, which the world considers to be foolishness. Chapter 4 summarizes the arguments of this study by illustrating the development of Luther's view of the gospel after Heidelberg: How was the Heidelberg Disputation a paradigmatic outline of future Protestant theology? An appendix containing Martin Bucer's letter about the disputation and a glossary of key terms are also included.

Plowing Hard Ground: What Others Have Taught Us

Jacques Barzun observed, "In the flood of material within even one field, the scholar is overwhelmed. The time is gone when the classical scholar could be sure that he had 'covered the literature' of his subject, the sources (once) being finite in number."[10] I have felt this overwhelming sense when writing on Martin Luther, for the sources seem to be unending. However, in focusing on the disputation itself and its immediate context, the sources available in English are significantly reduced. Gerhard Forde noted in 1997 that "the disputation has never received the comprehensive commentary that it deserves."[11] The following list of available sources seeks to share some of the scholarship available for the study of the Heidelberg

[10] Barzun, *From Dawn to Decadence,* 63. Parentheses added.

[11] Gerhard O. Forde, *On Being a Theologian of the Cross: Reflections on Luther's Heidelberg Disputation, 1518* (Grand Rapids: Eerdmans, 1997), 20. Since then, Fortress Press has published Dennis Bielfeldt's annotations (2015, see below), which give considerable help in interpreting the whole disputation.

Disputation—and how this present work has been helped by the men who have plowed hard ground for our benefit. A brief description of each work is also given.

The main primary sources provided for us are as follows: *Disputatio Heidelbergae Habita* and *Probationes*, found in *D. Martin Luthers Werke* 1, Weimar, 1883, 353–374. This was specifically helpful in studying Luther's teaching on grace (viz., the word *infusa*). "*The* Heidelberg Disputation and *Proofs*," Harold Grimm (trans.), found in *The Annotated Luther, Volume 1: The Roots of Reform,* was the main text used for the study of the disputation itself. Luther's *Disputation against Scholastic Theology,* presented on September 4, 1517, revealed more explicitly Luther's objections against scholasticism. This provided much help in learning the context of the disputation. Philip Melanchthon, *Loci Communes 1521*[12] was also used. Written three years after the Heidelberg Disputation, this work offered much aid in seeing how the early Lutheran Reformation viewed scholastic theology as well as key figures such as Aquinas, Biel, Scotus, and Aristotle. Another key primary source used in seeing the influences made upon Luther in 1518 was Augustine's *On the Spirit and the Letter* (discussed at length in chapter 2), which ran concurrently with Luther's thought expressed at Heidelberg. Aristotle's *Nicomachean Ethics* was also used, since it is the nexus that connects Luther's critique with the scholastics.

Regarding secondary sources, critical to interpreting the 1518 disputation is a knowledge of Martin Luther's personal spiritual development from around 1505 up to 1519. What were his early definitions of *faith, justification, righteousness*, and other terms, such as *theology of the cross*? When was his famed "evangelical breakthrough"? Lowell Green's *How Melanchthon Helped Luther Discover the Gospel* offered answers to these questions. In his "Historical Prolegomena," Green interacted with divergent theories regarding the date of Luther's evangelical breakthrough. In reading Luther's 1545 *Preface* to his collected Latin works,[13] Green concluded that

[12] Philip Melanchthon, *Commonplaces: Loci Communes 1521*, ed. and trans. Christian Preus (St. Louis: Concordia, 2014).

[13] WA, 54:179–187.

the breakthrough occurred between the years 1518 and 1519.[14] Later in the book, Green specifically targeted the breakthrough as occurring shortly before January 1519.[15]

Chapter 2 discussed the "Catholic" Luther, covering the years 1509 to 1518. As this title suggests, Green believed that these years found Luther still having vestiges of a Roman Catholic view of salvation and justification. While in general agreement with Green, I conclude that while the disputation is quite *Augustinian*, and therefore "Roman Catholic" in some respects, the disputation also clearly moved away from the mainstream of Catholic theology by asserting that salvation is entirely in Christ alone, with little to no mention of "cooperation."[16] The disputation, therefore, is a transitional piece. Green himself agreed: "We shall have occasion to see, however, that Luther's theology in the spring of 1518 was in transition and that the views reflected there (at Heidelberg) conflict with his mature understanding of Law and Gospel"[17] In chapter 3, Green addressed Luther's pre-Reformation understanding of justification—an understanding that was based on a theology of humility. Green's book ends by discussing how Melanchthon helped Luther grow in having a more forensic understanding of justification.

While Green gave much direction to rightly interpreting Luther's early years, Dennis Bielfeldt's introduction and annotations to the Heidelberg Disputation, found in *The Annotated Luther, Volume 1: The Roots of Reform,* proved to be invaluable to studying the disputation itself. In October 2015, Bielfeldt also wrote "The Philosophical Theses and Demonstrations of the Heidelberg Disputation." This paper helped in navigating the complex waters of the philosophical theses (29–40) by providing background in Aristotelian philosophy and Luther's interaction with it.

Another influential work was Joseph E. Vercruysse's 1976 journal article, "Luther's Theology of the Cross at the Time of the Heidelberg Disputation." His article traced the history of Luther's

---

[14] GREEN, 38.

[15] Ibid., 172.

[16] Cf. following quote, where Alister McGrath agrees.

[17] Ibid., 43. Parentheses added.

use of the phrase *theology of the cross* up to 1518. He noted that the phrase is complex, not straightforward.[18] The most important way this article informed the research was by his discussion of God's alien and proper work (*opus alienum* and *opus proprium*). This unlocked the disputation's main flow of argument and helped in understanding its overall structure as well.

Any work on the Heidelberg Disputation must encounter Alister McGrath's 1985 book, *Luther's Theology of the Cross: Martin Luther's Theological Breakthrough*. While not focusing on the entire disputation, McGrath's work addresses Luther's theology of the cross and gives background material to the disputation itself. The goal of his book is to be "an investigation of the development of Luther's doctrine of justification over the years 1509–1519, viewed in particular relation to his late medieval theological context."[19] He associates the theology of the cross quite closely to the doctrine of justification: "To indicate the manner in which Luther's developing insights into man's justification *coram Deo* are encapsulated in the concept of the 'theology of the cross.'"[20] Part I considers Luther to be a late medieval theologian. Here McGrath covers the *via moderna*, the study of the humanities, and the Church's prevailing soteriology. He contends that Luther was not a follower of the *via moderna*; rather, like Wittenberg at its beginning, he mostly embraced the *via antiqua* while also being influenced by the modern Augustinian school.[21] In Part II, McGrath discusses Luther's evangelical breakthrough. Citing Luther's writings before Heidelberg, he asserts that Luther's doctrine of justification—viz., its alien nature—differs from Augustine's at this time and that he lays the groundwork for Melanchthon's work in the future on forensic justification: "This concept of justifying righteousness is, of course, totally different from that of Saint Augustine, as Luther himself fully appreciates. This element of Luther's thought would be developed by Melanchthon into a doctrine of forensic justification, which would become normative for

[18] VERC, 525.

[19] TOCM, 2.

[20] Ibid., 2.

[21] Ibid., 30, 38, 68.

Protestant understandings of justification. Luther does not develop such a doctrine here, although it is clear that he lays a foundation for anyone who might care to undertake such a development."[22]

Another key article that gives insight into Luther's theology of the cross after Heidelberg is Robert Kolb's essay, "Luther's Theology of the Cross Fifteen Years after Heidelberg: Lectures on the Psalms of Ascent."[23] Kolb traces Luther's use of the phrase *theology of the cross* through his career, giving more detailed definition to terms, especially as they appeared after Heidelberg. His essay also gives broad treatment to the themes of the Heidelberg Disputation, which proved to be a great help.

Two final works that need to be discussed by way of literature review are Walther von Loewenich's *Luther's Theology of the Cross* (1976), and Gerhard O. Forde's 1997 book, *On Being a Theologian of the Cross: Reflections on Luther's Heidelberg Disputation, 1518.* Loewenich focuses on theses 19–20, giving commentary to Luther's doctrine of "the hiddeness of God." On the whole, Loewenich locates the Heidelberg Disputation as being part of Reformation Luther (and not "pre-Reformation" Luther): "This disputation belongs to the clearest and most basic statements of Luther in our possession."[24] He points out that antispeculation was a large part of Luther's early theology.[25] Loewenich discusses the hidden God as He appears in Luther's 1525 work, *The Bondage of the Will.*[26] He then gives significant attention to Luther's doctrine of faith in chapter 2.2. The discussion is important yet difficult. In chapter 3, he identifies the theology of the cross as being the center of Luther's entire theology, impacting each locus.[27] The theology of the cross is suffering, and "the Christian's glory consists exclusively in this weakness and

---

[22] Ibid., 134.

[23] Robert Kolb, "Luther's Theology of the Cross Fifteen Years after Heidelberg: Lectures on the Psalms of Ascent," *Journal of Ecclesiastical History* 61, no. 1 (January 2010).

[24] TOCL, 13.

[25] Ibid., 30.

[26] Ibid., 31–38.

[27] Ibid., 113.

lowliness."[28] Like Green, he sees Luther's early definition of faith as being humility[29] and focuses in chapter 3 on *the believer's* suffering and work rather than on that of Christ. Loewenich also compares and contrasts Luther's theology of the cross with mysticism, demonstrating how they are different.

In Gerhard Forde's *On Being a Theologian of the Cross*, he seeks to pastorally teach and apply the Heidelberg Disputation to a modern audience. He writes because (1) not much has been written on the Heidelberg Disputation, (2) any teaching on it has been sentimentalized and therefore misunderstood, and (3) he sees a serious erosion of theology in our lack of precise language.[30] For example, today we speak of ourselves as victims rather than sinners.[31] Forde's work is a devotional work rather than that of historical theology. He acknowledges this and humbly notes that more thorough work needs to be done in commenting on the entire disputation.[32]

Except for Green and Bielfeldt, each of these works—those of Vercruysse, McGrath, Kolb, Loewenich, and Forde—focus on theses 19–24, thus narrowing the discussion to Luther's categories of "theologian of glory" and "theologian of the cross." Of course, such focus is important to the study of Luther, and each of these men rightly chose to narrow their study to these themes. After all, even shortly after Luther's time, the category of the theology of the cross was seldom used.[33] However, while these works focus on theses 19–24, this essay has sought to give exposition to the entirety of the disputation with the interest of locating the theology of the cross within the disputation's broader argument and categories of Law, sin, grace, faith, and so on.

---

[28] Ibid., 118.

[29] Ibid., 129.

[30] Forde, *On Being a Theologian*, vii–ix.

[31] Ibid., x.

[32] Ibid., 20.

[33] Robert Kolb, "Luther on the Theology of the Cross," *Lutheran Quarterly* 16 (2002): 444.

Summary

In early 50 AD,[34] the apostle Paul set his sights to the western horizon as he left Athens, a city of great intellectual and philosophical power, to come to Corinth, a city of immorality, trust in wisdom, sophistry, rhetorical flourish, and immense pride.[35] "Corinth was a city where public boasting and self-promotion had become an art form."[36] It was a city of prostitution, a city that belonged to Aphrodite, a goddess who could be manipulated by sexual activity.[37] In short, Corinth was a wall of power. However, as the apostle approached the city, he determined to carry only one arrow in his arsenal: the arrow of the "weak" and "foolish" message of the cross.

The message was weak and strange. He came placarding a God who died helpless on a Roman cross to save the world. The message was a direct assault on human wisdom:

> For the word of the cross is foolishness to those who are perishing, but to us who are being saved it is the power of God. For it is written, "I will destroy the wisdom of the wise, and the cleverness of the clever I will set aside." Where is the wise man? Where is the scribe? Where is the debater of this age? Has not God made foolish the wisdom of the world? For since in the wisdom of God the world through its wisdom did not come to know God, God was well-pleased through the foolishness of the message preached to save those who believe.[38]

Corinth, as well as Luther's world and our world today, considered the message to be foolish. It cut across any vestige of human pride and any effort that a person would seek to give to God. It was a message that asserted that every person on earth was a bankrupt and

---

[34] Gregory J. Lockwood, *1 Corinthians* (St. Louis: Concordia, 2000), 15, fn. 85.

[35] Anthony C. Thiselton, *NIGTC: The First Epistle to the Corinthians* (Grand Rapids: Eerdmans, 2000), 12–15.

[36] Ben Witherington, in ibid., 13.

[37] Lockwood, *1 Corinthians*, 5–6.

[38] 1 Corinthians 1:18–22, *New American Standard Bible* (La Habra: Lockman Foundation, 1960, 1995). Italics added. This version is used throughout this book.

ungodly sinner: "For while we were still helpless, at the right time Christ died for the ungodly" (Rom. 5:6). It was a message that was a scythe, so to speak, in the hands of God, laying flat all the earth. As Paul wrote in Romans, "Now we know that whatever the Law says, it speaks to those who are under the Law, so that every mouth may be closed and all the world may become accountable to God" (Rom. 3:19). The wisdom of the world could not know God. And such wisdom considered the word of the cross foolishness. Yet the apostle Paul considered this word of the cross alone to be the power of God.

On the way to Corinth, Paul made a conscious and determined decision to know nothing, preach nothing, and say nothing to a city of power except the message of Jesus Christ and Him crucified (1 Cor. 2:2). As quoted earlier, Paul was certain of how God was not and how He was revealed: "For since in the wisdom of God the world through its wisdom did not know God, God was well-pleased through the foolishness of the message preached to save those who believe."[39] On his way to Heidelberg in 1518, Paul's conviction that God is not known by human wisdom but is revealed through the cross found a home in Martin Luther's heart. It was this conviction that Luther desired to untangle from the medieval and scholastic world that the conscience and well-being of Europe may be kept safe.

[39] 1 Cor. 1:21.

2
Context
On the Way to Heidelberg

Introduction

Eleven months before he traveled from Wittenberg to Heidelberg in 1518, Martin Luther wrote to John Lang, the prior of Erfurt: "Our theology and Augustine are progressing well and with God's help rule at our university. Aristotle is falling from his throne and his final doom is only a matter of time. It is amazing how lectures on the *Sentences* are disdained. Indeed, teachers cannot expect any students unless they teach this theology, that is, lecture on the Bible, St. Augustine, or another famous teacher of the church."[1] Unknown to Luther at the time, the triumphal tone of this letter (written even before the *Ninety-Five Theses*) would find its echo in the university walls at Heidelberg the following April.

A few months before journeying to Heidelberg, Luther presented his *Ninety-Five Theses, which* caused an uproar, specifically due to his attack on indulgences. In the spring of 1518, he was invited to defend his theology to the Augustinians in Heidelberg at their triennial meeting. He chose to not mention indulgences at all but rather to do what others had done at these gatherings: simply defend

[1] Scott H. Hendrix, *Martin Luther: Visionary Reformer* (New Haven: Yale University Press, 2015), 56.

the theology of Augustine. He also went to give a report of his work as district vicar.[2]

On April 11,[3] Luther began his journey on foot from Wittenberg southwest to Heidelberg accompanied by Leonhard Beier, who would present the disputation on Luther's behalf. On April 18, they arrived at Würzburg, which was 260 miles from Wittenberg. From there, they traveled another 100 miles until they arrived at Heidelberg on April 21 or 22. While traveling, Luther had on his mind the bramble of medieval errors that entangled the gospel message—a thicket he hoped to cut through by use of a disputation.[4] The goal of this chapter is to consider the events and ideas that surrounded Luther as he traveled to Heidelberg that one may understand what errors he was seeking to remove from Paul's message of the cross. The developments of Luther's personal life, theology, and Augustinian influence are also considered.

1. Aristotle

One cannot understand medieval theology or the Heidelberg Disputation without encountering the philosophy of Aristotle (384–322 BC).[5] Thus attention is directed to what Aristotle taught,

---

[2] James M. Kittelson, *Luther the Reformer: The Story of the Man and His Career* (Minneapolis: Fortress Press, 1986), 110. Martin Bucer described Luther's demeanor at Heidelberg: "Luther responds with magnificent grace and listens with insurmountable patience." Ibid., 112. See the appendix for Bucer's complete letter.

[3] Hendrix, *Visionary Reformer*, 69. The information for the following description of Luther's journey to Heidelberg is from Martin Brecht, *Martin Luther: His Road to Reformation 1483–1521* (Philadelphia: Fortress Press, 1985), 213–218, and Hendrix, 68–71.

[4] Cf. the glossary for definition of "disputation."

[5] For general background concerning Aristotle, the following sources were used: Aristotle, *The Nicomachean Ethics*, trans. David Ross (Oxford: Oxford University Press, 2009); Colin Brown, *Christianity and Western Thought: A History of Philosophers, Ideas and Movements* (Downers Grove: InterVarsity Press, 1990); Kelly James Clark, Richard Lints, James K. A. Smith, eds., *101 Key Terms in Philosophy and Their Importance for Theology* (Louisville: Westminster John Knox Press, 2004).

with special emphasis on his view of human nature and its interaction with ethics. Then discussion will be given to the question of why Luther disliked Aristotle, calling Aristotle (in Luther-like fashion), "a 'destroyer of pious doctrine,' a 'mere Sophist and quibbler,' an 'inventor of fables,' 'the stinking philosopher,' a 'billy goat' and a 'blind pagan.'"[6]

Aristotle's Philosophy and Ethics

Aristotle taught that the ultimate *telos* of human life was happiness—that is, a life that functioned properly, a life well lived. Such a life was accomplished through contemplation. "For man, therefore," wrote Aristotle, "the life according to reason is best and pleasantest, since reason more than anything else *is* man. This life, therefore, is also the happiest."[7] Presupposed in Aristotle's thought is the belief that human nature is good—that is, it is able to produce virtue by one's own will. One became virtuous by developing and repeating the right habits: "But the virtues we get first by exercising them, as also happens in the case of the arts as well. For the things we have to learn before we can do them, we learn by doing them, e.g. men become builders by building and lyre-players by playing the lyre; so too we become just by doing just acts, temperate by doing temperate acts, brave by doing brave acts."[8]

Another critical aspect of Aristotle's philosophy that is germane to Luther and the Heidelberg Disputation is Aristotle's view of *iustitia*—that is, justice or righteousness. In book V of *Nicomachean Ethics*, Aristotle's idea of justice is presented. Those who conduct just acts are just, while those who conduct unjust acts are unjust. One develops a just character by performing just actions. Justice and righteousness is something earned, something one can achieve by choice. "The just, then," wrote Aristotle, "is the lawful and the fair, the unjust the unlawful and the unfair . . . Since the lawless man was seen to be unjust and the law-abiding man just, evidently all lawful acts are in a

6 Brown, *Christianity and Western Thought*, 148.

7 NIC, book 10.7, 196. Italics are in the original.

8 Ibid., 2.1, 30–1103b, 23.

sense just acts; for the acts laid down by the legislative art are lawful, and each of these, we say, is just."[9] Luther and Aristotle agreed on the existence of the category of justice, yet they meant different things. Notice that according to Aristotle, a "legislative act" (a law originating from human reason) is lawful rather than God's holy Law (which originates from God). God's Law alone reveals the truth of human nature; Aristotle's law only speaks of righteous conduct. For Aristotle, such justice is complete "because he who possesses it can exercise his virtue not only in himself but towards another also."[10]

Luther and Aristotle

Luther's exposure to an Aristotelian education began as early as before 1502 at the University of Erfurt. He studied a commentary on Aristotle by Porphyry, Aristotle's *Analytics* and *Posterior Analytics*, and Aristotle's physics and psychology in his undergraduate years. For his master's, he studied Aristotle's *Topics*, his *Metaphysics* for six months, *Nicomachean Ethics* for eight months, and *Politics* for six.[11] "On the basis of this course of instruction," Martin Brecht wrote, "we can immediately recognize Aristotle's overwhelming significance for the study of philosophy. This extended even in theology." One Erfurt professor noted, "Without Aristotle no one becomes a doctor of theology."[12] After beginning his teaching career, Luther lectured on Aristotle's *Ethics* in the year 1508.

How did Luther react to Aristotle's philosophy? Alister McGrath outlines four key areas where Luther opposed Aristotle.[13] First, Luther understood Aristotle's view of reason as producing only a works-righteousness. "As Karl Holl pointed out, the God who answered to reason could never be anything other than the God of a 'works-righteousness,' who rewarded man on a *quid pro quo* basis."[14]

---

[9] NIC, book 5, 81.

[10] Ibid., 82.

[11] Brecht, *Martin Luther,* 33, 34.

[12] Ibid., 34.

[13] TOCM, 136–141.

[14] Ibid., 137.

Second, Luther thought reason was sufficient in God's left-hand kingdom (the kingdom of this world and its civil authorities and the use of pure reason), but reason was insufficient for God's right-hand kingdom.[15] "Theology is concerned with the affairs of heaven and philosophy with those of earth: for theologians to become philosophers is comparable to the birds of the air becoming the fishes of the sea."[16] Third, Aristotle's concept of God is false—an observation made by Luther's fellow Augustinian Hugolino of Orvieto.[17] Finally, Luther's vitriol seems to be uniquely directed against Aristotle's *Ethics*, which he observed the scholastics using to teach that God rewards the righteous only,[18] the righteous man is only the one who keeps the law, righteous deeds produce a righteous life (rather than vice versa, as Luther observed), and Aristotle's *iustitia* (mentioned earlier) went against Paul,[19] Augustine, and the entirety of Scripture. "In Luther's opinion," McGrath wrote, "reason was not neutral in this matter: according to reason, God should only justify those whose deeds made them worthy of such a reward."[20] Again, Luther's concern here is how the scholastics misused Aristotle and his teaching on reason, bringing him into the realm of theology.

Luther saw once again that God could not be known through Aristotle's emphasis on reason and his psychology (i.e., his view of human nature), which built on mere reason. Aristotle was concealing the knowledge of God from the world—especially as Aristotle

---

[15] For a detailed discussion on God's left-hand and right-hand kingdom, cf. William J. Wright, *Martin Luther's Understanding of God's Two Kingdoms: A Response to the Challenge of Skepticism* (Grand Rapids: Baker Academic, 2010), 117–142.

[16] TOCM, 138.

[17] Ibid.

[18] "God" under Aristotelian metaphysics did not give reward. Dr. Gregory E. Ganssle, professor of philosophy at Biola University and Talbot Theological Seminary, e-mail correspondence, May 30, 2017. Yet Luther's complaint was that the scholastics had used his reasoning to teach merit or reward for salvation.

[19] Though Aristotle's *iustitia* was not about a righteous standing before a holy God.

[20] TOCM, 141.

was being appropriated by scholastic theology. What was needed to recover the Christian message was an abolishing of Aristotelian philosophy. In such an abolition, God would be revealed.

2. Scholastic Theology

A second issue Luther sought to engage that he might safeguard the gospel was that which was the pervasive teaching of the medieval church: scholastic theology. As previously asserted, Luther saw the main error of scholasticism as being its synthesis with Aristotle, a synthesis that introduced works into the question of salvation. This section will briefly describe key components of scholasticism.[21] Luther's response to scholasticism will then be presented.

Thomism

Named after the great medieval theologian Thomas Aquinas (c. 1225–1274), Thomism is summarized by Dennis R. Janz in the following six tendencies: First, Thomism "posited a fundamental harmony between faith and reason." Reason can be used to argue for the existence of God and other matters of prolegomena. Yet it cannot demonstrate the truths of God's special revelation. Second, both nature and grace have their origins in God; therefore, there is continuity between the two. "Grace builds on rather than subverts or destroys human nature." Thus merit is affirmed while remembering that such merit is based on grace. Third, the final end (or telos) of human happiness is the vision of God. Fourth, "God would not have become incarnate had Adam not sinned." Fifth, the doctrine of Mary's Immaculate Conception is rejected. Finally, Thomist theology after Aquinas became increasingly more papalistic—especially after the Council of Constance.[22]

---

[21] Luther's life also encountered to some degree other aspects of scholastic thought, such as Albertism and Scotism. For example, Scotus's Pelagianism was often noticed and condemned by Luther as well as Melanchthon in his 1521 *Loci Communes*.

[22] Denis R. Janz, "Late Medieval Theology," in *The Cambridge Companion to Reformation Theology*, ed. David Bagchi and David C. Steinmetz (Cambridge:

Nominalism / Via Moderna

Lewis Spitz notes that the founder of the *via moderna* was William of Ockham (1280–1349), who noted that universals are merely symbols that do not exist outside of the human mind. This came to be known as nominalism. In nominalism, "faith and knowledge are far from each other and . . . it is impossible to base faith upon reason."[23] Unlike the realism of Aquinas and the Thomists, the *via moderna* declared that God was free to act any way He wished, stressing the omnipotence of God to the point where He needed no defense of human reason. The Word of God was supreme. God could have been saved by becoming a pickle if He so chose. God is free in His absolute power to do anything He chooses to do (*potentia absoluta*). Yet this was distinguished from God's ordained or regulated power (*potentia ordinata*), where God "actually does what He has chosen to do."[24] Along with distrusting human reason, nominalism also distrusted speculative theology—something scholasticism at large emphasized.

Perhaps the most well-known nominalist that is germane to the Heidelberg Disputation is Gabriel Biel (c. 1420–1495), who epitomized nominalism's semi-Pelagian development. Biel's thought on human nature and its relation to God's grace is summarized by the famous dictum "*faciente quod in se est, Deus non denegat gratiam*—'God does not deny grace to the man who does his best.'"[25] Biel's semi-Pelagian thought was very influential to medieval theology and pervasive in Luther's world by 1518. Therefore, he is quoted here in fuller length that one may better understand the theological winds that blew against Luther as he journeyed to Heidelberg:

Cambridge University Press, 2004), 7. Certainly, Aquinas taught much more than these six points. And later Thomists would disagree with him on points. There was also more nuance in Thomism than this brief outline suggests. Yet for the sake of brevity, these six points are very helpful in describing Thomism and its intersection with Luther.

[23] Lewis Spitz, *The Renaissance and Reformation Movements, Volume 1* (St. Louis: Concordia, 1971, 1987), 45.

[24] Ibid., 45, 46.

[25] TOCM, 60.

> You ask what it means for a man to do what is in him. Alexander of Hales answers as follows. 'If we want to know what it means for one to do what is in him, let us first note that every man by nature possesses right reason. The uprightness of reason consists of a natural understanding of what is good. It is given to every man by the Creator, and by its very soul can know its origin, God, . . . It knows further that it should seek the good from its Creator, that all men should beg what they still lack from their Origin. If a man acts in accordance with this innate knowledge and directs his will to him (God) . . . then he does what is in him . . .' From this we can now say that say that he does what is in him who, illumined by the light of natural reason or of faith, or of both, knows the baseness of sin, and having resolved to depart from it, desires the divine aid (i.e., grace) by which he can cleanse himself and cling to God his maker. To the one who does this, God necessarily grants grace.[26]

Speculation and Artificial Distinctions

The speculation and artificial distinctions that Luther observed in scholasticism flow from scholastic theology in general. Such distinctions would result in the obfuscation of life-giving doctrine, resulting in a theology of human wisdom that kept God from being known. Just three years after Heidelberg, Melanchthon gave concise expression to this tragic effect: "When once everything in the Scriptures began to be restricted to external works (a scholastic distinction based on reason), all Scripture was obscured, and lost was the understanding of what sin is, what grace is, what the Law is, what the Gospel is, what Moses is, and what Christ is. And this darkness, worse than that which was imposed on Egypt, we owe to the godless and cursed philosophy of the Scholastic pseudo-theologians."[27] With the heightened use of reason came many subtle theological definitions. For example, basic theological categories such as sin, grace, works, and so on were subdivided into

---

[26] Carter Lindberg, ed., *The European Reformations Sourcebook* (Oxford: Wiley and Sons, 2014), 14.

[27] Philip Melanchthon, *Commonplaces: Loci Communes 1521*, ed. and trans. Christian Preus (St. Louis: Concordia, 2014), 59. Parentheses added.

mortal sin, venial sin, works of congruity, works of condignity, works of supererogation, and so on.[28]

Religion of Merit

The culminating fruit of scholastic theology was a religion of merit—simply put, keeping God's Law and doing works to earn salvation. In the religion of merit, mankind was justified before God by works. This can be illustrated by the doctrine of purgatory in Luther's time.[29] Carlos Eire summarizes three theological assumptions that accompanied purgatory: "First, most Christians led less-than-exemplary lives; second, a lifetime on Earth was not sufficient to cleanse one from the stain of sin or to pay the penalties owed to God; and third, God could not require absolute moral perfection from the fallen human race. God's mercy demanded that there *had* to be some chance beyond this life to make up for one's failings."[30]

The example of Gasparo Contarini and his friends also serves to juxtapose the medieval religion of merit with grace. In 1510, a group of men (of whom Contarini was one) had a great concern for holiness and salvation. One of the men, Paolo Giustiniani, sought salvation by becoming an ascetic monk. Giustiniani's efforts seemed to be working, for Contarini despaired that he could never be as sacrificial as Giustiniani and his other friends. Yet his friends doubted their own salvation. "If his friends doubted whether they could ever atone for their sins by leading lives of austere piety," McGrath observed, "what

---

[28] The category of "faith," for example, was turned into at least nineteen distinctions: *fides actualis, fides apprehensiva, fides carbonaria, fides formata, fides caritate formata, fides directa, fides divina, fides humana, fides implicita, fides informis, fides iustificans, fides qua creditur, fides qua iustificat, fides quae creditur, fides reflexa, fides specialis, fiducia cordis*, and finally, *fiducia*, which simply means "trust." Richard A. Muller, *Dictionary of Latin and Greek Theological Terms* (Grand Rapids: Baker Academic, 1985, 1995), 116–118.

[29] Remarkably, though Luther eventually rejected the doctrine of purgatory, he still believed in some form of purgatory even shortly after Heidelberg. Cf. under "Luther's Personal Development."

[30] Carlos M. N. Eire, *Reformations: The Early Modern World, 1450–1650* (New Haven: Yale University Press, 2016), 136.

hope could there be for Contarini, who had chosen to avoid such a life by remaining in the world?"[31] Around Easter 1511, Contarini's spiritual blockage was obviated by grasping the finished work of Christ. "Even if I did all the penances possible," Contarini reflected, "they would not be enough to atone for my past sins . . . (Christ's) passion is sufficient, and more than sufficient, as a satisfaction for sins committed."[32] Though Contarini never left the Roman Church, he found a way to escape from his friends' religion of merit.

Luther and Scholastic Theology

Regarding the intricacies of medieval scholastic theology, even Luther's future nemesis Erasmus groaned, "One might sooner find one's way about a labyrinth than through the intellectual mazes of the Realists, Nominalists, Thomists, Albertists, Occamists, Scotists."[33] By 1518, Luther had developed a disdain for scholasticism because he saw it as obscuring and undermining the gospel message. Some have observed that Luther misunderstood scholastic theology.[34] Whether Luther's assessment of scholastic theology was accurate, we do not need to be in doubt *as to why* Luther rejected it. The year before Heidelberg, on September 4, 1517, Luther wrote his *Disputation against Scholastic Theology*. In this work, he attacked scholasticism's Aristotelian presuppositions (theses 40–45): "We do not become righteous by doing righteous deeds, but, having been made righteous, we do righteous deeds. This is in opposition to the philosophers" (40). "Indeed, no one can become a theologian unless he becomes one without Aristotle" (45). He takes aim at John Duns Scotus and Gabriel Biel for their high view of the human will: "It is false to state that the will can by nature conform to correct precept. This is said in opposition to Scotus and Gabriel" (6). "Man is by nature unable to want God to be God. Indeed, he himself wants to be God, and does not want God to be God" (17). "On the part of

[31] TOCM, 10.

[32] TOCM.

[33] Spitz, *Renaissance and Reformation Movements*, 46.

[34] E.g., VERC, 541.

man, however, nothing precedes grace except indisposition and even rebellion against grace" (30). "It is not true that God can accept man without his justifying grace. This is in opposition to Ockham" (56).[35] Luther attacked, in short, scholasticism's presuppositions, view of works, the will, and justification.

Harold Grimm gives a summary of Luther's concern with scholastic theology: "Ockham and Biel believed that man by nature could will to love God above all things and prepare the way for God's saving grace. Since, according to them, Christ's work of atonement became operative only after man had proven himself worthy of it, Luther could not be certain that he would be saved. Such certainty came only with his discovery of justification by faith alone."[36] It was this certainty that Luther wanted to carry with him to Heidelberg.

3. Mysticism

Along with Aristotle and scholastic theology, the development of mysticism was a third component of the context of the Heidelberg Disputation. Due to its very nature, mysticism was difficult to define, for it was experience-driven and very subjective, thus meaning different things to different people. However, Lewis Spitz gave a simple description of the mysticism of Luther's day. It was an intuitive and emotional appeal to spiritual reality, rather than having spiritual experiences based on the objective Word of God.[37] He states that mysticism is the belief that "the ultimate nature of reality or the divine essence may be known by the mystic through immediate apprehension, insight, or intuition."[38] In this apprehension of the divine, "the mystic experiences union or intercourse with the divine being in vision, in trance, or by absorption."[39] It is a union with God through ecstatic contemplation. Mysticism stressed perfectionism and love as being greater than reason.

---

[35] AE, 31.9–15.

[36] Ibid., 6.

[37] Spitz, *Renaissance and Reformation Movements,* 38.

[38] Ibid.

[39] Ibid.

Loewenich noted that mysticism had an emphasis on suffering, following the cross, annihilation, trial, and resignation to the will of God.[40] He observed that mysticism did not have a place for substitutionary atonement, for guilt was not the central issue. "The most serious lack in mysticism, strictly speaking, is that there is no place for the idea of guilt. For that reason it does not know what to do with forgiveness and atonement."[41] Perhaps all mysticism could be summarized with the importance of humility: humility before God, Christlike humility before the world. Famous mystics were Bernard of Clairvaux (1090–1153), Johannes Eckhart (1260–1327), Thomas à Kempis (c. 1380–1471) and the Brethren of the Common Life, and most importantly of all to Luther, Johannes Tauler (c. 1300–1361), whose book *A German Theology* Luther had published the same year as the Heidelberg Disputation. In this publication, Luther praised the work as a noble little book: "No book except the Bible and St. Augustine has come to my attention from which I have learned more about God, Christ, man, and all things."[42]

Martin Luther, Mysticism, and the Heidelberg Disputation

How did Martin Luther interact with mysticism in 1518? One can see his respect for it by the publication of Tauler's book and his lifelong appreciation of Bernard[43] (whom Luther considered to be a preacher of grace and whom he often referenced). He appreciated, for example, their emphasis on humility and the love of God, faith over reason, and their desire to resign oneself to the will of God. As will be shown, Luther had a strong "theology of humility," especially in his early career, which was reinforced by

---

[40] TOCL, 156.

[41] Ibid., 150.

[42] AE, 31.75.

[43] "According to Bernard the soul does not rest apart from Christ's wounds," Luther wrote. Quoted as an example of Luther's "passion-mysticism" in Volker Leppin, "Luther's Roots in Monastic-Mystical Piety," in OX, 52. "Luther then seized upon a unique accent of Bernardine mysticism, essentially a suffering mysticism, in that for Bernard the entire life of Christ appeared as suffering." Ibid.

mystical writing.[44] Some of mysticism's themes overlapped with the Heidelberg Disputation. For example, as will be seen in chapter 3, a significant part of the disputation's argument taught the need for the sinner to come to the end of himself by God's alien work. One is to be annihilated of his own efforts.

Yet the Heidelberg Disputation was a move away from mysticism. While the disputation had some overlapping concepts with mysticism, it was a message that was more focused on justification and the cross. First, while mysticism stressed an *immediate* knowledge of God through inner, subjective experience, the disputation stressed a knowledge of God through the *mediate* Word of God. Loewenich summarized this difference: "Here the ways between Tauler's mysticism and Luther's theology of the cross clearly separate. Theology of the cross is theology of revelation, while for mysticism the historical revelation is only a preliminary step to a direct, unbroken, and unmediated intercourse between God and the soul."[45] In the disputation, the Word of God is the greater authority over experience. Second, such immediate knowledge of God is an unvarnished theology of glory, where God is known in His majesty and glory rather than through the atoning work of Christ.

Third, "Luther rejects the speculative elements of mysticism, which constitute the indispensable presupposition for Tauler's mysticism, even in its ecclesiastically mitigated form."[46] Fourth, the Heidelberg Disputation addresses guilt and forgiveness by the work of Christ through faith alone, whereas classic mysticism focused on one's experience, minimizing the category of justification.

4. Augustine and *On the Spirit and the Letter*

Thus far, this chapter has surveyed Europe's theological landscape by giving attention to Aristotle, scholastic theology in its varied forms,

---

[44] Loewenich asserts that Luther developed his theology of the cross apart from his reading of Tauler. It was after he developed this theology that he found a "kindred spirit" in Tauler. TOCL, 153. Loewenich's argument seems plausible. Yet Luther's view of the primacy of humility was reinforced by mystical writings.

[45] Ibid., 155.

[46] Ibid., 156.

and mysticism. Yet woven through the fabric of medieval theology was the ever-pervasive issue of the nature of man and justification as outlined eleven centuries earlier by Augustine (354–430). Luther, of course, gravitated toward Augustine's teaching, and in the preface to the disputation, he asserted that Augustine is Paul's "most trustworthy interpreter." Augustine's themes of pride and humility also found resonance in Luther and affected his presentation at Heidelberg as well as his later theology. "For Augustine says very correctly," said Luther in 1531, "pride is the mother of all heresies; indeed, as both sacred and profane history testifies, it is the source of all sin and ruin."[47] Augustine's assertion of pride and humility, especially as related to justification, was expressed in his work from 412 AD against Pelagianism called *On the Spirit and the Letter*. This work also outlined Augustine's anthropology and doctrine of sin, grace, and justification. It was the chief work that Luther referenced in his proofs.

On the Spirit and the Letter was written to combat the Pelagian view of nature and grace, showing that grace was necessary and sovereign in order that humans might be justified before God. In chapter 5, Augustine wrote, "A man's free will, indeed, avails nothing except to sin . . . God's 'love is shed abroad in our hearts,' not through the free will which arises from ourselves, but 'through the Holy Ghost, which is given to us.'"[48] The Law without the Spirit only kills.[49] The Law can only reveal sin:[50] "When, indeed, He by the law discovers to a man his weakness, it is in order that by faith he may flee for refuge to His mercy, and be healed."[51] Sovereign mercy comes first to the sinner, making him beautiful: "He (God) does not, indeed, extend His mercy to them because they know Him, but that they may know Him; nor is it because they are upright in heart, but that they may become so, that He extends to them His righteousness, whereby He justifies the ungodly."[52]

---

[47] AE, 27.97.

[48] AUG, 84, 85.

[49] Ibid., chs. 6, 26.

[50] Ibid., chs. 16, 34.

[51] Ibid., chs. 15, 89.

[52] Ibid., chs. 11, 87. This is remarkably similar to thesis 28 of the HD.

Chapter 12 addresses pride and its relation to grace. In chapter 13, grace is clearly juxtaposed against works and merit. Grace comes through the Spirit's "assisting and healing."[53] The gospel, thus, leaves no room for boasting.[54] Pride comes from works that are done apart from faith,[55] a point Luther also made. Regarding grace and "the righteousness of God" (*iustitia*), chapters 15, 18, and the end of 31 present Augustine's view. The righteousness of God is "not that whereby He is Himself righteous, but that with which He endows man when He justifies the ungodly."[56] "It is called the righteousness of God, because by His bestowal of it He makes us righteous."[57] "'That we might be made the righteousness of God in Him.' This is not righteousness whereby God is Himself righteous, but that whereby we are made righteous by Him."[58]

Chapters 52 and 54 discuss the issue of the will. Augustine uses the phrase "free will," yet one's free will does not reside in man's nature apart from grace; free will must be given by a sovereign act of God. The Law brings knowledge of sin leading to faith, which leads to grace and healing. This healing leads to free will, which leads to love of righteousness that accomplishes the Law.[59] "But as the apostle says: 'There is no power but comes from God . . . for it is God who gave us even to believe.'"[60]

After reading *On the Spirit and the Letter*, one is struck by how often Augustine's work finds resonance in the Heidelberg Disputation. In chapter 1, we asserted that Luther in 1518 was still very Augustinian, yet he was also beginning to become more forensic than Augustine. Had he merely repeated Augustine's doctrine of justification at Heidelberg, why would he be met with opposition

---

[53] Ibid., chs. 13, 88.

[54] AUG, chs. 17, 21.

[55] Ibid., chs. 21, 22.

[56] Ibid., chs. 15, 88, 89.

[57] Ibid., chs. 18, 90. Here the righteousness of God seems to be righteous, ethical conduct.

[58] Ibid., chs. 31, 96.

[59] Ibid., ch. 52.

[60] Ibid., chs. 54, 107.

from the Erfurt professors? To be sure, they resented Luther's attack on Aristotle; however, more was being said than mere Augustinian theology. He clearly had touched a nerve by going beyond Augustine.

5. Luther's Personal Development

A final area to consider in thinking about the context of the Heidelberg Disputation is Luther's own personal development. What was his understanding of the gospel by the time he journeyed to Heidelberg? The years 1513 to 1521 found Luther assiduously studying the Bible as he prepared and gave lectures on Psalms, Romans, Galatians, Hebrews, and Psalms again.[61] It was during this time that Luther began to encounter his famed evangelical breakthrough.

Toward the end of his life, Luther reflected on these years as the time when he came to understand the gospel. "Then I began to understand that the righteousness of God (justitia Dei) is that by which the righteous live by a gift of God, that is, by faith, and that the Gospel reveals that a merciful God justifies us by faith with a passive righteousness . . . This made me feel as if I had been born again and passed through open doors into paradise itself."[62] His years of trying the medieval scheme of merit and monastic vows to gain salvation came to an end as he realized that one was saved by faith alone in Christ alone.

When did this happen? Scholars legitimately defend differing views. Some, such as Scott Hendrix and Alister McGrath, say this event happened as early as 1515.[63] After thorough examination of the evidence, Green asserts that the breakthrough occurred shortly

---

[61] Dates and events from Hendrix, *Visionary Reformer*, 27–98.

[62] Quoted in Eire, *Reformations*, 145.

[63] "Luther's insight came gradually during the year 1515, when he was preparing and delivering his lectures on Romans." Hendrix, *Visionary Reformer*, 52. Alister McGrath also sees Luther's conversion being in 1515. TOCM, 98. Regarding Luther's testimony from his p*reface* quoted earlier, McGrath states, "The preface in no way demands us to conclude that Luther's new theological insights took place in 1519, although it does clearly imply that they were complete by that date." TOCM, 145.

before January 1519.[64] However, another possible view of Luther's evangelical breakthrough was that it occurred not in one moment of time but rather as a slow and sure dawning over the course of years. The evidence suggests he had some understanding of grace and salvation being only in Christ alone in his 1515 lectures on Romans (see Hendrix, previously). In 1516, he wrote to George Spenlein a letter that sounded remarkably clear on the gospel. To Spenlein, who was in agony over the state of his soul, Luther wrote of Spenlein's need to come to the end of trying to find righteousness in himself and find it in Christ alone—"the immaculate righteousness of God which is freely given us in Christ."[65] However, in this same letter, Luther confesses to his own need to grow in understanding the gospel: "For my part, I am still wrestling with this error (the error of trying to find something good in himself) and am not quite rid of it yet."[66]

Just a few days before leaving for Heidelberg on March 31, 1518, Luther wrote to Staupitz,[67] "I teach that people should put their trust in nothing but Jesus Christ alone, not in their prayers, merits, or their own good deeds."[68] His trust in Christ alone is evident in 1516 as well as before and during Heidelberg. Yet he is still learning; the lens is continuing to be focused and sharpened. After returning to Wittenberg from Heidelberg, Luther published his *Explanations of the Ninety-Five Theses* at the end of August 1518.[69] Remarkably, in this work he still defends purgatory,[70] showing that his clarity on the gospel is still dawning and developing into its final form.

This observation that Luther's understanding of the gospel did not happen in a moment but slowly over time is important because the Heidelberg Disputation occurred during this development. We

---

[64] GREEN, 172. Also, cf. chapter 1 under "Literature Review."

[65] C. F. W. Walther, *The Proper Distinction between Law and Gospel* (St. Louis: Concordia, 1929, 1986), 109, 110.

[66] Ibid., 110. Parentheses added.

[67] While Hendrix states that Staupitz was the recipient, Brecht is doubtful. Cf. Brecht, *Martin Luther*, 213, 214.

[68] Hendrix, *Visionary Reformer*, 68.

[69] AE, 31.80.

[70] Ibid., 31.126.

shouldn't expect perfect clarity but rather should see the Heidelberg Disputation as a document that captures his soteriology in progress. We should not make it say too much, reading his future theology into it. Yet we should not discount it and make it say too little, as though it is merely another piece of Roman Catholic theology. It is a beautiful gospel treatise in nascent form.

Another significant component of early Luther was his theology of humility. Carl Trueman has noted that the theology of humility "involved the individual acknowledging their hopeless sinfulness before God and accepting the justice of God's condemnation upon them. Then, seeking no longer to assert the self over against God or as a basis for approaching God, the individual should approach God in a spirit of humility and of self-condemnation: such a one will find that God is gracious."[71] This was found in Luther's lectures on the Psalms as well as in the Heidelberg Disputation. As with Augustine and the mystics, emphasis was placed on humility before God. This theology of humility is most noticeably evident in his sentence, "*Crux sola est nostra theologia,*" found in his 1519–1521 lectures on the Psalms (*Operationes in Palmos*), as well as in his use of *theologia crucis,* found four times in his spring 1518 works against Eck, lectures on Hebrews, work against indulgences, and in the Heidelberg Disputation. It was also found in his *Operationes in Palmos* (mentioned earlier).[72] These phrases meant that the cross—that is, human suffering—leads one to despair of oneself and to look to God.

Summary

On his way to Heidelberg, Luther desired to do more than simply meet with a group of monks for theological discussion. He wanted to respond to the grave errors and *a priori* assumptions he noticed in the Church's theological world by going back to Paul and Augustine. "What he offered his fellow monks in Heidelberg," Robert Kolb observed, "was not a treatment of a specific biblical teaching or two.

---

[71] Carl Trueman, "Luther and the Reformation in Germany," in *The Reformation World,* ed. Andrew Pettegree (London: Routledge, 2000), 77.

[72] VERC, 524.

He presented a new conceptual framework for thinking about God and the human creature."[73] Luther fought against scholasticism and speculative theology as well as aberrant facets of mysticism. In going back to Paul, the Christian message would be disentangled from scholasticism, its ensuing religion of merit, and the uncertain and subjective elements of mysticism. The gospel would be safeguarded, with the result being a conscience kept safe from the demands of the Law through simple trust in Christ alone. The tenuous scaffolding of the scholastic system would be dismantled—and thus a blow given to human wisdom—while the genuine Christian message would be shared, revealing the true and living God.

---

[73] Robert Kolb, "Luther on the Theology of the Cross," *Lutheran Quarterly* 16 (2002): 443.

3
Exposition

"Distrusting Completely Our Own Wisdom . . ."

Introduction

Having considered Luther's personal life and theological world in 1518 (chapter 2), a better exposition of the disputation may now be given, allowing the work to speak to us from its original context. The intent of this chapter is to present a commentary on the Heidelberg Disputation. Most of the focus will be given to the theological theses (1–28), while the philosophical theses (29–40) will be more broadly summarized.

Luther's intent was to show the nature of true theology and thus how God was revealed. His concern was that people would clearly and simply believe in Christ, resting from their own works. He sought to accomplish this by moving his audience from discussion of God's necessary alien work (*opus alienum*) to His all-sufficient proper work (*opus proprium*).[1] True wisdom understands that the Law of God is to thunder from heaven and lay us low (God's alien

---

[1] *Opus alienum* is God's alien work of wrath and judgment—works that do not seem proper to the being of God. Yet these works are the penultimate servant of God's ultimate work for the sinner—His *opus proprium*, whereby Christ comes to the convicted and humbled sinner full of nothing but grace and promise and the forgiveness of sins, bringing free salvation (cf. Richard A. Muller, *Dictionary of Latin and Greek Theological Terms* [Grand Rapids: Baker Academic, 1985, 1995], 214; and VERC, 530, 531).

work) and thus lead us to forsake any self-righteous work and trust in Christ alone, where He comes with nothing but sweet grace to the sinner (God's proper work). Like Paul, he defined the world's wisdom—human wisdom—as trying to gain salvation by works and thinking of God in terms of human reason; this was foolish, causing one to be a theologian of glory (1 Cor. 1:21). And, like Paul, he saw the wisdom of God as "calling a thing what it is," telling the truth about man's depravity, God's wisdom, and the grace of Christ found in the cross alone (1 Cor. 1:23–25)—the theology of the cross. The forty theses of the disputation are outlined as follows: the truth about works, the truth about the human will, obtaining grace, true wisdom, righteousness and faith, the truth about God's love, and human wisdom and the wisdom of God.[2]

1. The Truth about Works (1–12)

In the first twelve theses, Luther showed the holiness of the Law and yet its impotence in bringing about righteousness for sinful man. To trust in works of the Law was to be plunged into "mortal sin" and ultimate condemnation. In these theses, he clearly addressed the importance of God's alien work in bringing a person to true knowledge of God and to true faith in Christ.

Thesis 1 confronts the inability of one to be justified by the Law: "*Thesis 1: The law of God, the most salutary doctrine of life, cannot advance human beings on their way to righteousness, but rather*

[2] For a similar outline, cf. Joseph E. Vercruysse, "Gesetz und Liebe: die Strutur der 'Heidelberger Disputation' Luthers (1518)," *Lutherjahrbuch* lxviii (1981): 7–43, referenced in Dennis Bielfeldt, *The Philosophical Theses and Demonstrations of the Heidelberg Disputation,* henceforth PT (Institute of Lutheran Theology, October 2015), 3. Also, Martin Brecht's outline: the works of men and of God (1–12), the anthropological foundations of human activity (13–18), understanding God's action (19–24), the relationship of faith and works (25–27), the love of God (28), and the philosophical theses (29–40), which assert that Aristotle had been misunderstood by the scholastics and was worthless apart from Christ—"a perverse passion of the mind" if not accompanied by Christ and His grace. Martin Brecht, *Martin Luther: His Road to Reformation 1483–1521,* trans. James L. Schaaf (Philadelphia: Fortress Press, 1985), 231–235.

hinders them." The Law,[3] specifically the Decalogue, is to be an external and holy help from God yet fails because of human nature. In his proofs, Luther referenced Paul's teaching in Romans 5:20, 8:2, and 2 Corinthians 3:6, and concurred with Augustine, showing how the Law incites sin. The problem lay not in the Law, but in man—specifically, man's heart. How, then, can it advance a person on to righteousness before God? It cannot, for man's heart is only wicked. The beauty and splendor of the Law laid before a dead man cannot elicit a response. Instead, it can only incite the rebel heart to war against the Law. Luther's opening thesis is a jarring salvo that alerts the reader to the alien work of God.

Against Pelagian and semi-Pelagian thinking, thesis 2 confronts the inability of natural man to do works of righteousness: "*Thesis 2: Much less can human works, done over and over again with the aid of 'natural principle' (as it is called), lead to that end.*" If the holy Law of God from heaven cannot help a person to live a righteous life, then how much less can a person's own natural propensity help? In thesis 1, Luther cut the soul off from any help from the Law. In thesis 2, Luther eviscerated any hope a person might have in himself to live a righteous life before God. "If persons do not do good with help from without," Luther said, "they will do even less by their own strength."[4] As seen in chapter 2, this was a direct confrontation to Aristotelian ethics (which taught that man was naturally good and could simply choose correctly) or to scholasticism's encouragement to "do what lies within you."

Thesis 3 reveals human works for what they are—damning sins if one relies on them for righteousness: "*Thesis 3: Although the works of human beings always seem attractive and good, it is nevertheless probable that they are mortal sins.*" Human works of the Law seem attractive and radiant. The medieval church was replete with examples of men such as the Carthusians who sacrificed that they might earn salvation. Yet these works are filthy, polluted, and

---

[3] RR, 88. Luther agrees with Augustine that the law is "every law, even the holiest law of God." Bielfeldt observed that Luther's use of "law" was against that of Jerome and Erasmus, who considered Paul's use of law to be only ceremonial. RR, 89, note 36.

[4] RR, 89.

self-serving.[5] To trust in such works would be a true mortal sin, a *peccata mortalia*—"sins that result in damnation and eternal death because their commission so denies faith and the work of the Spirit that salvation becomes impossible."[6] They are mortal sins because, in the end, they are simply a trust in one's own righteousness. They are done without being united to Christ by faith alone. In his proofs, Luther compares these works to the Pharisees, which look fine on the outside but are dead on the inside.

Thesis 4 observes that God's alien works seem unattractive and evil; yet in truth, such works are rich in splendor and life-giving to those who have been humbled by them: "*Thesis 4: Although the works of God always seem unattractive and evil, they are nevertheless really immortal merits.*" Here Luther is speaking of God's alien work of humbling a person and stripping away the apparent luster of human works. Thesis 4 is a subtle foreshadowing of theses 19–24, where Luther's well-known theology of the cross is discussed. God's alien works "always" seem unattractive and evil—especially when compared to the seemingly iridescent works of man described in thesis 3. God seems to hide in what appears to bring destruction on our lives. Yet such works of God are in truth "really immortal merits." That is, they produce true humility and the fear of the Lord. "The Lord humbles and frightens us," Luther said regarding this thesis, "by means of the law and the sight of our sins so that we seem in human eyes, including in our own, as nothing, foolish, and wicked, for we are in truth that."[7]

Scholars have rightly observed that at this point in Luther's life (1518), he had a strong theology of humility, discussed in chapter 2. He seemed to equate humility with faith and thus taught that one is almost justified by humility; humility/faith was considered to be an energizing substance that wrought practical righteousness as one

[5] Two years later, in 1520, Luther published *Treatise on Good Works* and *The Freedom of a Christian*. These works went into great detail to expose the folly of works done without faith alone in Christ. Such works were mere forms of idolatry and in violation of the first commandment, setting one up as one's own God.

[6] Muller, *Dictionary*, 220.

[7] RR, 90.

despaired of himself and turned to Christ.[8] Faith was letting God be God, not questioning His ways or wisdom, but trusting Him, though He may appear evil.[9] This stage in Luther's theological development is evidenced in his comment on thesis 4: "Humility and the fear of God are our entire merit."[10]

Thesis 5 affirms good works. However, it condemns good works if they are trusted in for salvation: "*Thesis 5: The works of human beings—we speak of works which appear to be good—are thus not mortal sins as if they were crimes.*" After the preceding theses, one may think that Luther condemned all good works. However, in this thesis, he does not consider good works to be ontologically mortal sins, "such as adultery, theft, homicide, slander, etc."[11] Yet these good works become mortal sins when they are trusted in for making one righteous before God.

Theses 6 and 7 continue to show the folly of self-righteousness and of trying to be justified by works, for even one's best works, done with God's help, are stained with sin. The righteous see things as they are; therefore, out of reverence for God, they acknowledge that their works are sinful and not to be trusted in for salvation: "*Thesis 6: The works of God—we speak of those that are done through human beings—are thus not merits as if they were sinless.*" Even the works of God done within us by union with Christ and by the Holy Spirit's enabling are not sinless. This is Luther's doctrine of *simul iustus et peccator* ("at once righteous and a sinner") making its appearance. The one who has been justified by faith alone is a true saint, fully just in God's sight and accepted as though he had perfectly kept the Law. Yet this same person is also still a sinner in practice. In thesis 6, Luther is confronting the scholastic error of thinking that our good works produced by the Spirit are spotless before God and can earn

---

[8] GREEN, 95. "Thus according to the young Luther, man, in justifying God through humility, justifies himself. Where humility dwells in the heart, there can only be a genuine relationship with God, bringing life and salvation. Humility is therefore nearly identical with faith."

[9] Ibid., 101.

[10] RR, 91.

[11] Ibid.

merit. "If someone cuts with a rusty and rough hatchet, even though the worker is a good craftsman, the hatchet leaves bad, jagged, and ugly gashes. So it is when God works through us, etc."[12]

"*Thesis 7: The works of the righteous would be mortal sins were they not feared as mortal sins by the righteous themselves out of pious fear of God.*" The works of the righteous become "mortal sins" if they are trusted. But the truly righteous distrust such works, for they see the truth of God's holiness and the folly of human works. They see the perfection of His Law and the infinite sinfulness of human nature. The righteous concur with thesis 6. Here Luther takes a swipe at the medieval distinction between mortal and venial sin and asserts that all sin—whether "mortal" or "venial"—is sin that damns one to hell.[13] The sin of works-righteousness is the truly mortal and damning sin that bars one from heaven.

Theses 8–10 consider works done without faith. If even a righteous person's works are not to be trusted (as thesis 7 taught), *how much less* should mere human works done without faith be trusted. To distinguish between different kinds of works, as did the scholastics, is to reject the fear of God and land one into carnal security. "Dead" works are not neutral (as the scholastics categorized); rather, they are damning: "*Thesis 8: All the more are human works mortal sins when they are done without fear and in unadulterated, evil self-security.*" If the works of the righteous are mortal sins (as thesis 7 states), how much more are human works—works done without faith and humble reverence for God. "*Thesis 9: To say that works without Christ are indeed dead but not mortal sins seems a perilous rejection of the fear of God.*" Further amplifying thesis 8, Luther asserts that works done without Christ are not just dead works; they are mortal, damning one for all eternity. They rob God of His glory. "How much more

---

[12] RR, 92. Bielfeldt notes that this same metaphor is used in the *Bondage of the Will*, written in 1525.

[13] In 1537, Luther wrote in his *Smalcald Articles* regarding the folly of distinguishing sin and thereby dodging our guilt: "Repentance does not debate over what is a sin or what is not a sin. Instead, it simply lumps everything together and says, 'Everything is pure sin with us.'" Robert Kolb and Timothy Wengert, eds., *The Book of Concord: The Confessions of the Evangelical Lutheran Church* (Minneapolis: Fortress Press, 2000), 318. This concurs with thesis 7 of the HD.

does that person offend him (God) who continues to withdraw glory from him and does this in complete security!"[14] "*Thesis 10: Indeed, it is very difficult to see how a work can be dead and at the same time not a culpable, or mortal sin.*" To call a work merely "dead" is to look at it as being neutral, neither good nor bad. We must either love or hate dead works. Given this choice, our evil natures will always love dead works that seem so impressive to the world yet are hideous before God.[15] This makes us culpable of "mortal sin"—specifically, the "mortal sin" of doing works not out of the honor for God.

In theses 11–12, Luther continued to dislodge his medieval and Renaissance world from any hope in human works and merit as one agreed with God about the truth of sin and the folly of works. Sins only condemn us when we are not emptied of the pride of works. "*Thesis 11: Arrogance cannot be avoided nor can true hope be present, unless the judgment of damnation is feared in every work.*" For Luther, true hope rested in realizing one's own best works only merit damnation. Thus humility once again comes into singular importance in his overall argument (see previous comments on thesis 4). One must completely despair of one's merits or anything in the creature before true hope can be gained. In his proofs for thesis 11, Luther wrote, "It is impossible to hope in God unless one has despaired regarding all creatures and knows that nothing can profit oneself without God."[16] "Hope" meant the beginning of dislodging one's confidence from self to Christ, a hope that would be based on *Christus in nobis*—Christ **in** us, transforming us—rather than Luther's later *Christus pro nobis*—Christ **for** us, resting in His finished work on the cross (and thus a soundly Melanchthonian view of imputation, which would be more fully developed after Heidelberg).[17] "*Thesis 12: As a consequence, in the sight of God sins are truly venial when human beings fear them as mortal.*" Here Luther is meeting the medieval distinctions of venial and mortal sins on their own field of play. If you want to speak of such distinctions, he seems to say, then very

---

[14] RR, 93. Parenthesis added.

[15] Ibid., 94.

[16] RR, 94.

[17] GREEN, 167.

well: Those sins that you think are mortal are in fact only venial, for they can be forgiven by sheer grace. God's pardon is in accord with our self-accusation as we see the utter inability of our works to justify. Through such self-accusation, sins do not damn us eternally; they are merely venial.

Summary of Theses 1–12

In contrast to scholastic theology and the medieval religion of merit, Luther was asserting in theses 1–12 that a true theologian sees mankind's performance of God's Law for what it is: worthless to justify a person before God. The fault lay not with the holy Law of God but rather with man's depraved nature that is incapable of performing the Law. In these theses, Luther applied God's *opus alienum,* tearing from humanity any hope of being righteous before God by works. He attacked the nuanced scholastic definitions of works and sin of any kind—works done in us by the Holy Spirit, works done without Christ, neutral works (dead works), works of congruity, works of condignity, venial sin, and mortal sin. Along with the apostle Paul, he is telling the truth about all humankind: that we are all sinners—even the most religious—and that any system that offers help in doing good works to attain salvation (such as the scholastic system did) is merely human wisdom: it is a ruse clothed in a faulty distinction of terms that are meant to assuage or evade guilt and to minimize the true nature of sin.

2. The Truth about the Human Will (13–15)

In theses 13–15, Luther continued his withering analysis of human nature and its inability to justify itself before God. In the following theses, he considered the truth about the nature of man's will; it is *not* free, Luther would declare. Therefore, the will was unable to choose righteous conduct or to even choose salvation that can justify a person. Theses 13–15 serve as a transition from the truth about human works (1–12) to the obtaining of grace (16–18). The entire argument of the disputation and the doctrine of justification is underpinned for Luther by the teaching that humans are so dead that even the will is in need of grace.

"*Thesis 13: Free will after [the fall into]*[18] *sin, exists in name only, and when 'it does what is within it,' it commits a mortal sin.*" In this thesis, Luther used the word *arbitrium*, rather than the word for "will" that Erasmus would later use, *voluntas.*[19] "The will (*voluntas*) is the faculty that chooses; *arbitrium* is the capacity of will to make a choice or a decision. Thus, the will can be viewed as essentially free and unconstrained but nonetheless limited by its own capacity to choose particular things and, in view of the restricting and debilitating effects of sin . . . , in bondage to its own capacities."[20] While Erasmus and the scholastics in general spoke of the faculty of the will being free, Luther spoke of the *arbitrio*—that is, the capacity of the will to choose righteousness or grace. This capacity was in bondage to sin and unable to respond to God. Erasmus spoke of the "power of choice"—in other words, the fact that humans have a will that chooses.

While Luther certainly recognized that humans have a will, he spoke of the will's *arbitrio*—that is, its affections and desires. Therefore, he said, the will is enslaved.[21] With this distinction in mind, we can see why he said in thesis 13 that free will "exists in name only." He also quoted Augustine from *On the Spirit and the Letter*: "Free will without grace has the power to do nothing but sin."[22] Therefore, our wills are incapable of even choosing grace. Since the will is in bondage and cannot take the first step in responding to God, how could one effectively follow Gabriel Biel's admonition? Free will is another idol for the self-righteous to worship and trust in order to justify oneself before God's Law. In thesis 13, Luther is simply continuing to strip a person of any vestige of hope in themselves that

---

[18] Parentheses added in English version. The original is *Liberum arbitrium post peccatum res est de solo titulo, et dum facit quod in se est, peccat mortaliter.* WA, 354.

[19] Erasmus and Luther's crossing of swords over the nature of the human will is discussed in chapter 4.

[20] Muller, *Dictionary*, 330, 331. Parentheses added.

[21] Scott Keith, "Creeds and Confessions," class notes (Christ College Irvine, CA, Summer 2016).

[22] RR, 95.

they may be truly led to God's proper work of bringing Christ to the humbled sinner.[23]

Theses 14 and 15 continued to develop Luther's understanding of the will by asserting that one is entirely dependent on God to incline the will to choose Him. "*Thesis 14: Free will, after [the fall into]*[24] *sin, has the power to do good only passively, but always has the power to do evil actively.*" After the fall, "free will" can only do good passively—that is, only when the will is acted upon from the outside by God alone. On its own—"actively"—the will can only do evil. Luther ended his *proof* for thesis 14 by appealing to Augustine's "various writings against the Pelagians,"[25] for Augustine knew that if the will could act righteously without grace, then Christ died for nothing and man could be his own savior. In short, the issue of the will could undermine the entire gospel if incorrectly taught.[26] "*Thesis 15: Nor in the state of innocence could free will remain an active power, much less make progress in the good, but remains in innocence only a passive power.*" Continuing the assertion of thesis 14 and continuing to cite Augustine, Luther asserted in thesis 15 that Adam (and his posterity) only had "passive power" in his state of innocence; that is, even in innocence, Adam was entirely dependent on God for any ability to obey.

Summary of Theses 13–15

In theses 13–15, Luther turned from the issue of works for attaining righteousness to the issue of the will. The wisdom of God calls the will what it is: a dead faculty, unable to contribute to salvation. He showed that the human will is dead to God, unable to respond unless acted upon by God's sovereign prerogative. He did not issue forth

---

[23] Bielfeldt interestingly notes that thesis 13 is the only one that was "explicitly condemned by the 1520 papal bull, *Exsurge Domini*." RR, 82, fn. 19.

[24] Parentheses added in English translation. Cf. WA, 354.

[25] RR, 96.

[26] This is Augustine's frequent appeal in his work *On Predestination*. Augustine did use the phrase "free will" often in his works (e.g., in *On Nature and Grace*); yet what he meant by this term was similar to Luther's teaching on the will.

such alarming doctrines to cause people to despair; rather, he did so that people may find hope in Christ alone.

3. Obtaining Grace (16–18)

Theses 16–18 continue to show the folly of man's works by further confronting Biel's encouragement to do what is in oneself and then trust God to make up for what is lacking. Luther shows the faulty engineering of such scaffolding; such grace cannot hold the weight of the Law's demands: "*Thesis 16: The person who believes that one can obtain grace 'by doing what is in oneself' adds sin to sin and thus becomes doubly guilty.*" Doing "what is in oneself" can only produce sin, for there is nothing in the nature of a sinner's heart that can yield righteousness, as theses 1–15 demonstrated. To do what is within only produces sin—especially the sin of self-righteous pride in one's works. Pride is heaped upon pride as "doing what is within" leads one farther and farther away from God and His grace, heaping guilt upon guilt. If all one can do is produce sin, how can our doing obtain grace? One may think of Contarini's quandary, discussed in chapter 2: How could doing what was in himself—specifically, living an ascetic life—atone for his sin? Contarini heaped on himself sin upon sin as he tried to obtain grace by his efforts. How would Luther urge his readers to respond to thesis 16? "Fall down and pray for grace and place your hope in Christ in whom is salvation, life, and resurrection."[27]

At this point, Luther continued to transition from God's alien work to His proper work: "The law humbles, grace exalts. The law effects fear, and wrath, grace effects hope and mercy. 'Through the law comes knowledge of sin' [Romans 3:20]; through knowledge of sin, however comes humility, and through humility grace is required . . . God makes a person a sinner so that he may make him righteous."[28] In this quote, all the themes of the disputation are being invoked. Also, he is teaching justification by humility. Although he still linked faith to humility, here there is still the core truth of the gospel: a person must look entirely outside of himself to Christ alone. Thesis 16 is the

[27] RR, 97.

[28] Ibid.

hinge of the disputation's argument, turning the helpless sinner to the joyous good news of Christ. This is beautifully shown in the next theses: "*Theses 17 and 18: (17) Nor does speaking in this manner give cause for despair, but rather for humility, for it arouses the desire to seek the grace of Christ. (18) It is certain that one must utterly despair of oneself in order to be made fit to receive the grace of Christ.*" The tragic facts of theses 1–16 are not meant to leave one hopeless and in the dust; rather, they are to lead one to look entirely outside of himself to the grace of Christ. Here for the first time is the guilty sinner led to the bright light of day, from the darkness of one's heart to the blinding splendor and joy of grace and hope in Jesus alone. Through the convicting power of the Law, one is led to truly seek the grace of Christ.

At the time of the disputation, Luther still had a more medieval understanding of the word *grace*. Along with Augustine's *On the Spirit and the Letter*, Luther considered grace to be an infused quality that enabled a person to do ethical or actual acts of righteousness. Grace was considered a disposition of soul rather than favored standing with God. Luther's definition of grace changed in 1521 after "taking up Erasmus's argument that the New Testament Greek word, *charis* (grace), means God's favor, not a disposition of the soul."[29] However, though Luther still had this undeveloped understanding of the word *grace*, we can see in the disputation his main concern: one must look entirely away from any work or goodness within to rest in a righteousness outside of us found only in Christ. With the coming of Melanchthon to Wittenberg around August 29 (the date of Melanchthon's inaugural address at the University of Wittenberg), Luther would gain greater focus and clarity concerning grace, specifically its forensic nature connected to the atonement. At this point, his expression of the grace of God is still Augustinian, yet he is beginning to move to the forensic.

Summary of Theses 16–18

Theses 16–18 are the hinge upon which the disputation moves Luther's argument from God's *opus alienum* to His *opus proprium*. He brings theses 1–15 to a concluding summary by asserting that one must look entirely away from any scholastic scheme of self-justification

[29] Ibid., 102, fn. 53.

through works to the work of Christ. The world considers such teaching to be the foolishness of God, yet only in such teaching is God revealed.

4. True Wisdom (19–24)

As observed in the first chapter, most scholarship on the disputation has focused on theses 19–24—specifically, the phrases "theology of glory" and "theology of the cross." Who can adequately grasp the depths of the paradox[30] of the wisdom of God—a wisdom the world deems to be foolish—and the wisdom of the world, which is foolishness to God? In this set of theses, Luther concisely captures Paul's doctrine and proclamation of the cross as it collides with the wisdom of the world. "*Thesis 19: That person does not deserve to be called a theologian who perceives the invisible things of God as understandable on the basis of those things which have been made [Rom. 1:20].*" One who seeks to understand "the invisible things of God"—"virtue, godliness, wisdom, justice, goodness, and so forth"[31]—and says these can be understood based on natural revelation cannot be teaching true and accurate theology, for this is void of the cross, the only way God has chosen to reveal Himself. This was the common approach of Aquinas. While remaining tethered to God and His special revelation (viz., the Scriptures), Aquinas sought to prove God's existence and ethics from natural law.[32] Natural theology that uses a human starting point will lie to us, for we are blinded by sin and a corrupt heart. Such theology is based on human reason. This thesis also begins to introduce theses 29–40, which address Aristotle's role in scholastic theology. Aristotle and human reason cannot ascend to heaven and see the invisible things of God. Rather, God must come

---

[30] "Paradoxes" (Latin: "Theologica paradoxa" [WA, 353]) is the word Luther used to describe these theses.

[31] RR, 98.

[32] Cf. Aquinas's writings on ethics and natural law in Robin Gill, ed., *A Textbook of Christian Ethics* (London: Bloomsbury Publishing, 2014). Also, cf. Dr. Jeffrey Mallinson, "Christianity, Ethics, and Contemporary Culture," class notes (Christ College Irvine, CA, Fall 2015).

down to us through the foolishness of the cross (1 Cor. 1:18). It is here alone that God is revealed.

"*Thesis 20: The person deserves to be called a theologian, however, who understands the visible and the 'back side' of God [Exod. 33:23] seen through suffering and the cross.*" A true theologian finds God revealed *only* in the cross—specifically, in the suffering and crucified Christ: "True theology and knowledge of God are in the crucified Christ, as it is stated in John 10 [John 14:6]: 'No one comes to the Father, except through me.'"[33] Concerning this thesis, Luther wrote, "The 'back' and visible things of God are placed in opposition to the invisible, namely, humanity, infirmity, foolishness, etc. The Apostle in 1 Cor. 1[:25] calls them the weakness and folly of God."[34] He made reference to Moses being only allowed to see the backside of God.

Here Luther seems to associate the theology of the cross to the work of Christ, where God is manifested.[35] However, Luther's understanding of "the cross" in 1518 also referred to God's alien work. Vítor Westhelle noted that Luther's understanding of the atonement at this point was somewhere between Anselm's satisfaction model and Abelard's moral influence theory of the atonement. Luther avoided giving too sharp of a definition of the atonement at this time.[36] Westhelle also observed, as did Green, Vercruysse, Kolb, and others, that the phrase "theology of the cross" (*theogia crucis*) was used by Luther in his Hebrews lectures of 1517–1518, where Luther noted that God's opposing works are side by side: "Judgment and righteousness, wrath and grace, death and life, evil and good. This is what is referred to in the phrase . . . 'And alien work is done by him so that he might affect his proper work' . . . Here we find the 'Theology of the Cross,' or, as the apostle expresses it: 'The word of the cross is a stumbling block to the Jews, and foolishness to the Gentiles' [1 Cor. 1:18,23], because it is utterly hidden from their eyes."[37]

---

[33] RR, 99.

[34] Ibid.

[35] Here the theology of the cross is not simply Luther's *Crux sola est nostra theologia*.

[36] Vítor Westhelle, "Luther's Theologia Crucis," in OX, 158.

[37] Ibid., 158.

In this thesis, Luther harkens again to 1 Corinthians 1 and God's destruction of the wisdom of the wise through His "foolish" message: "Now it is not sufficient for any, and it does them no good to recognize God in his glory and majesty, unless they recognize him in the humility and shame of the cross."[38] In this sentence, Luther is taking aim at two groups. First, he is confronting the scholastics by asserting that God destroys our efforts to relate to Him by righteous works and scholastic and philosophical speculation. He also takes a perhaps inadvertent swipe at the mystics who believed that God could be seen and *immediately* known (as opposed to *mediately* known through Christ and the cross) in His essence.[39] This thesis, in summary, affirms Paul's argument in 1 Corinthians 1 that God cannot be known by earthly wisdom and reason—that is, by our works. Instead, He can only be known through the wisdom of God—that is, by "Christ Jesus, who became to us wisdom from God (1 Cor. 1:31)."[40]

"*Thesis 21: A theologian of glory calls evil good and good evil. A theologian of the cross calls a thing what it actually is.*" This thesis, perhaps more than any other, is the umbrella over the entire disputation and this essay as well. A theologian of glory calls evil good; that is, he calls works-righteousness and human merit a good thing. Yet as Luther demonstrated, these works are evil, for they have their root and origin in man, not in God. Describing the theologian of glory, Vercruysse wrote, "The theologian of glory pretends to have

---

[38] RR, 99.

[39] Though he did seem to confront the mystic error, Luther was still appreciative of the German theology, writing with praise the preface to Tauler's *Theologia Deutsch* in 1518. Just a few weeks before Heidelberg, Luther wrote to Staupitz on March 31 of his glowing appreciation of Tauler's work. OX, 57. He retained some aspects of mystical theology throughout his career while also sharpening his theology based on the objective work of Christ on the cross.

[40] Westhelle also helpfully noticed Luther's important idea of "the preached God" as being the only God one can know. We are not to know God apart from the preached promises in Christ. "This led Luther to make a sharp distinction between God in God-self, God's aseity, and God revealed in the Word, the 'preached God': 'God must be left to himself in his own majesty . . . it is no business of ours . . . [we must make] the distinction between God preached and God hidden, that is, between the Word of God and God himself.'" OX, 162.

direct access to God, present in glory and majesty, in wisdom and strength within the wise and powerful realities and deeds in creation: God's invisible wisdom, strength and goodness are visibly mediated in the created wisdom, strength and goodness which are as reflections of God's qualities, his glory and majesty. The recurrent reference to Aristotle and the likeness with the statements of the *Resolutiones* make clear that Luther thinks here especially of the scholastic approach."[41]

In contrast to the theologian of glory, a theologian of the cross sees sin, works, grace, human merit, and God's revelation accurately, from God's perspective. Vercruysse further described such a theologian: "The theologian of the cross is the sinner, the evildoer, the fool and weakling, the needy and poor man. He experiences God's love, which creates out of nothing what deserves love and makes, thus, the needy sinner righteous, good, wise, strong."[42] To not know God solely in the person of Christ and His suffering is to prefer works, human glory and strength, Aristotle, scholastic wisdom, and so on. Without knowing God as He is revealed on the cross, one cannot and does not know God: "The world through its wisdom did not come to know God" (1 Cor. 1:21). While scholars have done effective work in showing how Luther's theology of the cross affects one's way of seeing all the categories of the Christian faith, in thesis 21, the theology of the cross seems to be directly related to the issue of knowing God through being "made"[43] righteous in His sight—that is, justified.[44] He does mention general suffering in his proofs for thesis

---

[41] VERC, 537.

[42] Ibid., 539. This quote bleeds into a commentary on thesis 28. At first glance, Vercruysse here seems to misunderstand Luther when he writes, "What deserves love and makes, thus, the needy sinner righteous, good, wise, strong." Yet he is accurate, for in 1518, Luther's view of "grace" and "justification" were more factitive and directly Augustinian.

[43] "Made" is used instead of "declared," for in April 1518, Luther had not yet fully arrived at his forensic understanding of justification—though he was well on his way.

[44] In thesis 24, "theology of the cross" entails suffering that God brings to lead a sinner to despair of himself. As observed in chapter 2, this was a more common use of Luther's phrase.

21.[45] Yet the *telos* of his argument ends by showing how the message of the cross crucifies one's own efforts for *iustitia* (righteousness), rendering human effort as utter foolishness.

Theses 22–24 analyze the nature of the world's wisdom—specifically, the theology of the glory, where one tries to relate to God by works. "*Thesis 22: The wisdom which sees the invisible things of God in works as understood by human beings is puffed up, blinded, and hardened.*" "Wisdom" that seeks to see the invisible things of God in works (i.e., our works, our glory, our wisdom, etc.) is never satisfied; rather, such wisdom only results in further arrogance and hardness of heart. This arrogance and hardness of heart comes from the deception of trusting in one's own merits. Luther is restating the truth of thesis 16. Again, echoing Augustine's prime interest in humility and his disdain for pride,[46] Luther's concern is that all boasting would be in God alone. This is a sure and certain fruit of God's alien work and then His proper work. "*Thesis 23: The law works the wrath of God, kills, reviles, accuses, judges, and condemns everything that is not in Christ [Rom. 4:15].*" Human wisdom (trying to relate to God by works of the Law) can only bring condemnation. In this thesis, Luther returns to his teaching on the condemning work of the Law found in theses 1–12. In his proofs for this thesis, he discusses Paul's teaching of the curse the Law brings to lawbreakers (Gal. 3:10). Because humans have no righteousness and cannot render works that would justify one before God, the law can only kill those who are confident they are keeping the Law. After showing the impotence of trying to be justified by the Law, he quickly notes that this does not mean the Law is evil: "*Thesis 24: Yet that wisdom is not of itself evil, nor is the law to be evaded; but without the theology of the cross a person misuses the best things in the worst way.*" The Law is not evil; on the contrary, the Law is from God. Yet without the

[45] "To be sure, because they hate the cross and suffering, they love works and the glory of works." RR, 100.

[46] For example, cf. the opening paragraph to Augustine's *City of God*, where he asserts that there are only two cities in the world: the city of God, whose citizens are humble and characterized by love of God, and the city of man, whose citizens are proud and are characterized by love of self. God will crush the sons of pride.

theology of the cross, even the best things from the hand of God can only be misused. Here in thesis 24, the phrase "theology of the cross" goes back to Luther's teaching concerning God's alien work and his theology of humility: "The person who has not been brought low, reduced to nothing through the cross and suffering, takes credit for works and wisdom and does not give credit to God. That person thus misuses and defiles the gifts of God."[47]

Summary of Theses 19-24

As previously stated, this set of theses concisely captures Paul's wisdom of God found in the gospel message and its collision with the world's way of thinking. The world's wisdom says that humans have merit and can render works to make one righteous with God. God's wisdom says such thinking is folly. In Christ alone and through Christ alone can one truly know God. This destroys the speculation and superstition of the religion in Luther's day. A true theologian is a theologian of the cross, one who realizes the limit and folly of human wisdom, works, and reason and understands that God is freely revealed in Christ and the cross alone.

5. Righteousness and Faith (25-27)

In theses 1–12, we observed that the revelation of God is given to one who has faced the truth about the impotence of human works to be accepted by God. In 13–15, we saw that a genuine knowledge of God accepts the truth about the human will—that the will is not free, but is in bondage. Theses 16–18 asserted that true theology shows that the free grace of God comes only to those who have experienced God's alien work and hope in Christ. Theses 19–24 taught that God is known by a theologian of the cross who eschews all notions of glory. He finds God only as He is revealed in the person and work of Christ. This leads to theses 25–27, where the convicted sinner is brought to God's proper work of trust in the finished work of Christ alone.

---

[47] RR, 101.

"*Thesis 25: That person is not righteous who works much, but who without work believes much in Christ.*" While "righteous" here is more factitive than forensic, it is a more fully developed understanding of righteousness than Augustine's teaching and has forensic hints. "Without work" entails one coming to the end of oneself or his or her own efforts. It is to be humbled by God's alien work that one might then "believe much" in Christ; that is, that one may look entirely to Him and His work to make one righteous. "Believe" here as we have seen is more about being rightly humbled than it is about simple trust (though, of course, trust is involved). Green observes that Luther's understanding of hope and faith in April 1518 is not yet assurance or confidence. This came shortly after Heidelberg in August. At Heidelberg, Luther understood faith to be a substance—something that gains a reward and transforms a person. Throughout theses 25–27, this understanding of faith undergirds Luther's argument.[48]

Concurring with Augustine's teaching, Luther comments on this thesis, "For grace and faith are infused without our works . . . Thus, because people know that works done by such faith are not their own, but God's, therefore they do not seek to become justified or glorified through such works but seek God. Their justification by faith in Christ suffices for them, that is, Christ is their wisdom, righteousness, etc., as 1 Cor. 1[30] has it, but they may be Christ's action and instrument."[49] Here Luther teaches that grace is infused (*infusa* in the original). It is a substance, strength, or a disposition toward

[48] Green refers to Luther's assessment of faith before he met Melanchthon. Submitting to Jerome and Lombard, Luther's view before Melanchthon was faith as a substance. "Through faith Christ is our 'substance,' that is, our riches, and simultaneously we through the same faith are his 'substance,' that is, we are made a new creature." One can see how confusing Luther's definitions were! Yet after Melanchthon, Green observes of Luther's understanding of faith, "From now on faith would instead be 'assurance,' confidence, trust that God is favorable and forgiving. Faith would entail the certainty that the believer is at the present moment completely justified by the gracious verdict of God and that he has complete assurance of his eternal salvation." GREEN, 146, 147. It was the former view of faith that Luther carried with him to Heidelberg.

[49] RR, 102, 103.

God rather than a standing of favor with God. This goes along with Augustine's view of grace more than Melanchthon's (as well as Erasmus's; see above) view of grace being defined as favor.

Though Luther was more Augustinian when the disputation was presented in 1518, the point of thesis 25 overlaps with his later view of justification—namely, this: Our justification is entirely outside of ourselves and entirely in Christ alone and by Christ alone. It has nothing to do with our works or even our resolve. Like sharpening the focus of a camera lens, Luther would shortly after Heidelberg focus his understanding of grace, righteousness, and faith into a more Melanchthonian understanding of justification that is imputed and forensic. Justification would be more directly linked to an Anselmian view of the atonement—specifically, Christ as our substitute who took the entire wrath of God and the curse of the Law upon Himself that we might be freely forgiven.

Of course, it is impossible to know exactly what was in Luther's mind in April 1518 regarding this thesis. But based on the aforementioned evidence, he did seem to be closer to Augustine than Melanchthon. However, it is also probable that he had at least some idea of imputation in mind, for toward the end of his life, he maintained that he always had the same understanding of justification throughout his career as a reformer. In his 1537 Smalcald Articles on justification, he wrote, "I cannot change at all what I have consistently taught about this until now, namely, that 'through faith' . . . we receive a different, new clean heart and that, for the sake of Christ our mediator, God will and does regard us as completely righteous and holy. Although sin in the flesh is still not completely gone or dead, God will nevertheless not count or consider it."[50]

Theses 26 and 27 continue to further explain the relationship of faith, grace, and works. "*Thesis 26: The law says, 'Do this,' and it is never done. Grace says, 'Believe in this One,' and everything has already been done.*" Unfolding thesis 25, thesis 26 states that the works of the Law gain nothing. In his proof for thesis 26, Luther again appeals to Augustine's *On the Spirit and the Letter* and *On Nature and Grace.*

---

[50] Quoted from Mark Mattes, "Luther on Justification as Forensic and Effective," in OX, 264.

He continues to teach an infused understanding of grace—*Christus in nobis* rather than *Christus pro nobis.* "For through faith Christ is in us, indeed, one with us. Christ is righteous, fulfilling all the commands of God, wherefore we also fulfill everything through him if he has been made ours through faith."[51] Luther's view of "believe" at this point in his life was that belief (or faith) was a substance. Faith was humility or submission, where one comes to the end of himself.[52] Through dependence on Christ, the believer is united to Him and begins to do good works, where God alone receives the glory. "*Thesis 27: Properly speaking, one should call Christ's work an active work and our work a passive work, and thus the passive work is pleasing to God by the grace of the active work.*" Christ's work is an "active" work; that is, He acts upon us that we may work. Therefore, our work is a "passive" work that becomes pleasing to God by grace. "[Christ] now moves us to do good works through that living faith in his works."[53] His works serve as models for us.

Summary of Theses 25–27

Theses 25–27 move the reader into God's proper work, which brings the sheer good news of Christ, the news that nothing comes from us but everything comes from Him. While these theses are beautiful if seen in the light of Luther's developed theology, in 1518 they were still more Augustinian. However, there is significant overlap with Luther's later understanding of the gospel.

The true Christian message, Luther would say, is one that says farewell to the Law as a way to become righteous before God. Such work has no end and nothing gets done. Instead, the true theologian now simply believes in Christ—and in believing, all is done. This, and this alone, is how God is known. Human wisdom—that is, trying to know God by one's reason and by one's works—can never reveal the true and living God.

---

[51] RR, 103.

[52] Cf. GREEN, 95, 101. Also, cf. the glossary for the definition of "theology of humility."

[53] RR, 103.

6. The Truth about God's Love (28)

Having led the reader from God's convicting and condemning work to God's proper work of coming to the sinner by pure grace and the promise of forgiveness in Christ, Luther now turns to the true nature of the love of God—it is freely given to the unlovely, to those bankrupt of any good works of the Law: "*Thesis 28: God's love does not find, but creates, that which is pleasing to it. Human love comes into being through that which is pleasing to it.*" Luther saw in Aristotle's understanding of love a root that was simply love for the self—not an unconditional love for another: *Human love comes into being through that which is pleasing to it.* Aristotle's love was only toward objects that were worthy of love.[54] Aristotle taught that humans had a passive ability to love—that is, one's capacity to love was conditioned on a lovable object acting on one's faculty. Thus only that which was beautiful or worthy would be an object of another's love. Bielfeldt quotes Aquinas as a scholastic theologian who agreed with Aristotle on this matter: "Love belongs to the appetitive power, which is a passive faculty (*vis passive*). Wherefore, its object stands to it as the cause of its movement (*motus*) or act (*actus*). It is necessary, therefore, that the cause of love be, properly speaking, the object of love."[55]

Contrary to Aristotle and Aquinas, Luther observed from Scripture that God set His affection on that which was unworthy of love, on that which was unlovely. This is contrary to human wisdom. This simple truth cut against the entire medieval system of religion, where God's love and acceptance were given to those who were lovely through good works. "For this reason," Luther said, "sinners are attractive because they are loved; they are not loved because they are attractive. And for this reason human love avoids sinners and evil persons."[56]

In his proof for thesis 28, Luther seems to tie God's love and grace directly to the atonement. This is one of the places in the disputation[57] where he seems to begin to go beyond Augustine's factitive justification to a more forensic view of the atonement: "This is the love of the cross, born of the cross, which turns in the direction where it does not

---

[54] Cf. proofs for thesis 28, ibid., 104.

[55] RR, 104, fn. l. The quote is from *Summa Theologica* I–II, Q. 27, A1.

[56] RR, 104.

[57] Another place would be in thesis 6, which alludes to *simul iustus et peccator*.

find good, which it may enjoy, but where it may confer good upon the evil and needy person."[58] Luther moves salvation entirely away from any work inside of a person to the work that was done *for* a person in history. This work, then, justifies a person and brings forth good fruit.

Summary of Thesis 28

Thesis 28 stands alone in many ways, yet it is the final argument to his theological theses. There is nothing in the human heart that commends one to God. The heart is altogether corrupt and unlovely. Unlike the nature of human love, Aristotelian reasoning, and the scholastic scheme of merit, God's love falls on the unlovely and the undeserving. God then makes the unlovely beautiful. This is contrary to human wisdom, which tries to ascend to God by being lovely in works of the Law.

7. Human Wisdom and the Wisdom of God (29–40)

The last twelve theses of the disputation have often been overlooked. Yet for Luther, they were essential to the entire work, for in these theses, he confronted the underlying presuppositions of scholastic theology: its synthesis with Aristotle (as seen in chapter 2). With this synthesis, Luther believed the gospel and the revelation of God were lost. In short, all the categories of true theology became distorted. What was at stake was the Christian message and the threat of the wisdom of God being usurped by human wisdom. This concern was expressed in a letter Luther wrote to Jodocus Trutfetter shortly after Heidelberg, where he expressed to his former teacher what Luther considered to be the key issue of the disputation: "I simply believe it is impossible to reform the church, unless canons, decretals, scholastic theology, philosophy, logic, as we now have them, be eradicated completely and other studies substituted; . . . You may think I am no logician, and perhaps I am not, but this I know, that I fear no one's logic in defending this conviction."[59]

---

58 RR, 105.

59 Ibid., 79. Trutfetter was not pleased. Upon hearing of Luther's teaching on Aristotelian and scholastic thought at Heidelberg, he refused to allow Luther in his home when Luther sought to visit Trutfetter on his return from Heidelberg.

In theses 29–30, Luther considers the proper use of Aristotle. Theses 31–35 examine the fallacies and inconsistencies of Aristotle's causality. Theses 36–39 confront Aristotle's metaphysics. Thesis 40 seems to be a summary statement of Luther's analysis of Aristotle's teaching—a teaching that ultimately has form, matter, and ideas being the same. For Luther, this would ultimately infer that there is nothing higher than what is seen.

Theses 29–30 introduce the philosophical theses and summarize Luther's main argument concerning Aristotle and the revelation of God. "*Theses 29–30: (29) Whoever wishes without danger to philosophize using Aristotle must beforehand become thoroughly foolish in Christ (30). Just as no one uses the evil of lust properly unless married, so nobody philosophizes well unless a fool, that is, a Christian.*" Aristotle has his proper use. Use him, but only after embracing the foolishness of God through trust in Christ. Once again, Luther appeals to the apostle Paul's argument in 1 Corinthians 1: Only those who are foolish according to the world (because of trust in Christ and His cross) can truly use human wisdom or reason. As an unbeliever, even Aristotle could not use Aristotle correctly! Reason and philosophy have their right place and use, but only as they are submissive to the wisdom of God—specifically, the message of the cross where God is revealed. Regarding thesis 30, Luther wrote, "Just as lust is the perverse desire of pleasure, so philosophy is a perverse love of knowing, unless the grace of Christ is present. It is not that philosophy or pleasure is evil, but that, outside of Christians, the desire of either cannot be proper."[60]

Theses 31–35 teach us of Luther's understanding of Aristotle's causality. "*Theses 31–35: (31) It was easy for Aristotle to believe that the world was eternal since he believed that the human soul was mortal.*[61] *(32) After it was held [by Aristotle] that there are just as many substantial forms as composite ones, it was necessary to hold also that there are just as many material ones. (33) Nothing comes about necessarily from any particular reality in the world; nevertheless, necessarily whatever comes about*

[60] PT, 8.

[61] Aristotle thought that "perhaps" the human could possibly survive death (Dr. Gregory E. Ganssle, professor of philosophy at Biola University and Talbot Theological Seminary, e-mail correspondence, May 30, 2017.).

naturally, comes about from matter. (34) If Aristotle had recognized 'the absolute power of God,' he would have maintained that it is impossible for matter to exist unformed (nudam). (35) According to Aristotle, there is no actual infinite, yet with respect to potentiality and form there are as many infinities as there are composite things." In these theses, Luther writes what he sees as the flaws and inconsistencies of Aristotle's causality—and how such causality does away with immortality, "the absolute power of God," and thus man's accountability to God. In thesis 35, Luther observes that Aristotle's actuality and potentiality can go on forever: An acorn can be actuality *and* potentiality. An acorn's potentiality can become an oak tree (actuality), which can then become an acorn, and so on.[62] This can go on for infinity, thus going against Aristotle's view that there is "no actual infinite."[63] While Aristotle believed that the soul was mortal, Luther believed that Aristotle's own argument concluded that the soul was immortal. Regarding thesis 31, Luther saw that "Aristotle is committed to the view that matter, form, and their composite comprise one single thing. Since a human being is a corruptible composite, the soul,—which is part of the corruptible composite—is itself corruptible."[64] This brings us back to the overall message of this essay: Aristotle denies the revelation of God and therefore immortality; thus humans are left with only their own reason, which cannot know God.

Theses 36–39 address Aristotle's metaphysics. "*Theses 36–39: (36) Aristotle wrongly rebukes and lampoons the philosophy of 'Platonic ideas,' a philosophy that is better than his own. (37) The 'imitation of numbers' in things is cleverly asserted by Pythagoras, but cleverer still is the participation of ideas asserted by Plato. (38) The disputation of Aristotle (if a Christian will pardon this) 'fights against' Parmenides' idea of oneness 'by beating the air' [1 Cor. 9:26]. (39) If Anaxagoras posited the infinite before form [of things], as it seems he did, he was the best of the philosophers, even if Aristotle was unwilling to acknowledge this.*" Luther here asserts

[62] For discussion on Aristotle's metaphysics, cf. Marc S. Cohen, "Aristotle's Metaphysics," *Stanford Encyclopedia of Philosophy*, ed. Edward N. Zalta (Winter 2016), https://plato.stanford.edu/archives/win2016/entries/aristotle-metaphysics/.

[63] "If the past is eternal, then there is no 'actual infinite.' This is a problem for Aristotle" (Ganssle).

[64] RR, 77.

that even the errant philosophies of Pythagoras (who said, "All things are made of number"[65]) and Parmenides (who believed, like Aristotle, that all is one, yet unlike Aristotle, believed that the One is "beyond all things and nevertheless in all things"[66]) and Anaxagoras (who said that everything is made of everything, yet the mind is incorporeal[67]) are to be more esteemed than Aristotle. Luther commends Plato over Aristotle (thesis 37), for he taught ideas outside of and beyond matter. Aristotle's inseparableness of ideal and matter (unlike Plato, who separated them and thus "strives for the divine and immortal, separate and eternal," as Luther wrote[68]) leads to the foolishness of Aristotle's philosophy. "And so it appears," Luther concluded, "that the philosophy of Aristotle crawls in the dregs of corporeal and sensible things, whereas Plato moves among things separable and spiritual."[69]

"Thesis 40: To Aristotle, privation, matter, form, mobility, immobility, actuality, potentiality, etc. seem to be the same thing." Luther concluded Aristotle's categories to be the same. Regarding thesis 40, Bielfeldt summarized Luther's observation of Aristotle's epistemology thus: "Instead of looking towards the heavens to know the things of the world, the world is the basis upon which we can look to heaven."[70] Aristotle's thought reasoned from man to God, not vice versa.

Summary of Theses 29–40

Vítor Westhelle summarizes the importance of these philosophical theses: "Medieval standards for theology began with general philosophical assumptions—most often appealing to Aristotle—to establish the premises of natural revelation before special revelation could be presented . . . If the present-day reader were to take them up first, it would be clear that the philosophical theses provide

---

[65] Ibid., 88, fn. 33.

[66] Ibid., 88, fn. 34. Parmenides also believed that time and motion were illusions (Ganssle).

[67] Ibid., 88–89, fn. 35.

[68] Ibid., 87.

[69] Ibid.

[70] PT, 22.

the background for his basic argument in the theological theses."[71] Westhelle rightly argues that Luther wanted to bring an epistemological change to theology, where Scripture alone—that is, the special revelation from God—would be the starting place of theology rather than human reason. In these theses, he buttresses his central argument to the disputation: God is not known through human wisdom and one's efforts to ascend to God through reason. Rather, God is revealed through suffering and Christ and His work on the cross.

Concerning the philosophical theses, Gerhard Forde wrote: "The righteousness before God comes only by hearing and believing . . . Such righteousness can only appear shocking compared to the wisdom of an Aristotle . . . It is consequent then that the philosophical theses . . . are aimed at the Aristotelian premises undergirding a theology of glory."[72] The philosophical theses expose the Aristotelian presuppositions upon which scholasticism is built—presuppositions that undercut the fact that God is only revealed through suffering and the cross.

Summary of Chapter 3

For Luther, ultimately, the true Christian message—consisting of Law and gospel, faith and grace, the bound will's absolute dependence on God, and the "theology of the cross"—was to be presented in purity at Heidelberg, shorn of all its medieval trappings. Human wisdom, with all its misguided trust in one's works and its relating to God by sight rather than faith, was put in its place, while the truth that God is known only through His alien work of humbling the sinner and bringing him or her to the sweet promise of grace in Christ was given further clarity. True theology asserts that God is not known by human wisdom, but He is revealed through suffering and the cross. Luther's message at Heidelberg is further summarized by table 3.1.

The theses presented at Heidelberg were printed immediately, while the proofs were not published until 1530. Timothy Wengert gives a concise summary of the theses: "These terse antithetical

---

[71] Vítor Westhelle, "Luther's Theologia Crucis," in OX, 157.

[72] Gerhard O. Forde, *On Being a Theologian of the Cross: Reflections on Luther's Heidelberg Disputation, 1518* (Grand Rapids: Eerdmans, 1997), 105.

Table 3.1

Theses	Human Wisdom	"The Word of the Cross" That Reveals God
Works (1–12)	Works are "do-able" and enable one to reach God.	Works condemn us, for they cannot be done perfectly in accord with the majestic perfection of God's Law.
Human Will (13–15)	The will is sick but good; it can cooperate with God (Biel).	The will is dead and in bondage; it is not free.
Obtaining Grace (16–18)	Grace is given to those who work.	Grace is unmerited and freely given apart from any effort.
True Wisdom (19–24)	The cross is foolish. God must show Himself through power.	Christ and the cross alone are the wisdom of God.
Righteousness and Faith (25–27)	Righteousness is gained by observing the Law.	Righteousness is gained by nothing in us, but solely by Christ.
The Love of God (28)	God sets His love only on the lovely.	God sets His love on the unlovely and the unlovable.
Human Wisdom and the Wisdom of God (29–40)	Epistemology starts with human reason; God can be known solely by one's own reason.	Epistemology starts with revelation; God can only be known through suffering and the cross.

statements outline such quintessential, Luther-esque teachings as the distinction between law and gospel, the bondage of the will, justification by faith not works, and most celebrated today, the theology of the cross."[73] Such crisp definition would prove to be paradigmatic for Luther's mature thought on the gospel and for the theology of what would be known as the Reformation.

[73] Timothy Wengert, RR, 4.

4

Conclusion

Luther after Heidelberg

The Beginning and End of All Theological Thought

Toward the latter part of his career, Martin Luther wrote in his preface to the 1535 publication of *Lectures on Galatians*, "For in my heart there rules this one doctrine, namely, faith in Christ. From it, through it, and to it all my theological thought flows and returns, day and night; yet I am aware that all I have grasped of this wisdom in its height, width, and depth are a few poor and insignificant firstfruits and fragments."[1] By 1535, Luther's understanding of the gospel and its key terms that appeared in nascent form in the disputation had reached their full and matured expression; the "camera lens" of his understanding of the gospel had finally come into sharpened focus. The aim of this chapter is to summarize the findings of this study of the disputation by comparing the disputation with Luther's matured theology. This approach will help in gaining a better understanding of what the disputation said—and what it had not yet said.

Luther left Heidelberg to return to Wittenberg in late May or early June. He was encouraged by his time in Heidelberg and believed the younger participants responded well to his theses, while the older professors, such as Jodocus Trutfetter,[2] responded negatively to his

---

[1] AE, 27.145.

[2] Preserved Smith, trans. and ed., *Luther's Correspondence and Other Contemporary Letters, Vol. 1, 1507–1521* (Philadelphia: Lutheran Publication Society, 1913),

argument. "I have great hope that, as Christ, rejected by the Jews went over to the Gentiles, so this true theology of his, rejected by those opinionated old men, will pass over to the younger generation . . ."[3] Though not much opposition happened directly after Heidelberg, small clouds of the gathering storm of the Reformation were ominously sighted on Europe's horizon; thunder was heard over Leipzig in 1519 as Luther defended *sola scriptura,* and the storm finally broke during 1520 and 1521, when Pope Leo X issued his *Exsurge Domine* and Luther was excommunicated. The gospel of grace—specifically, justification by faith alone—was a storm front that crashed against the Church's religion of merit.

The preceding chapters have shown that the disputation was Luther's early understanding of the gospel. It was quite consistently Augustinian; yet the disputation began to go beyond Augustine and far away from scholasticism. Table 4.1 summarizes how the disputation had remaining overlap with the Roman Church. Table 4.2 summarizes how the disputation began to break away from scholasticism and move toward what would later be known as Protestant theology.

From Heidelberg to the end of his life, Luther's antipathy toward Aristotle and scholasticism remained unchanged. His argument expressed in theses 29–40 continued after Heidelberg. For example, in *Galatians*, he frequently condemned relating to God by human wisdom. He spoke of reason's desire to make men think well

Table 4.1

Remaining Aspects of Roman Catholicism in the Disputation
Grace is still defined as being *infusa* yet seems to *begin* to move away from Augustine to a more Protestant understanding of grace
Contains aspects of an Augustinian view of justification (more factitive)
Faith is primarily defined as humility
Remnants of an Abelardian understanding of the atonement (see glossary, "cross")

85. Also, cf. chapter 3, fn. 60. Luther also tells of his trying to persuade Dr. Usingen, who traveled with him in the wagon on the return journey: "I know not what success I had, for I left him pensive and dazed." Smith, 85.

[3] Ibid.

Table 4.2

Beginnings of Protestant Theology *(How the Heidelberg Disputation Breaks Away from Scholasticism)*
Salvation is entirely *extra nos* and alien
Works of the Law cannot bring one to know God
No place for works in the justification of sinners
Hints of an Anselmian view of the cross (yet still Abelardian, see glossary, "cross")
Complete break with Biel and the scholastic view of human nature
No language of "cooperation"
Categorically denies free will
Rejects Aristotelian presuppositions

of themselves and to thus undermine grace and the gospel: "In short, human reason would like to present to God an imitation and a counterfeit sinner, who is afraid of nothing and has no sense of sin."[4]

Luther distanced himself from mysticism (of which the disputation had hints) after Heidelberg. He moved from an emphasis on the subjective to an emphasis on the objective promise of Christ. He condemned the mystic impulse to have immediate knowledge of God.[5] One should "refrain from speculation about the majesty of God, which is too much for the human body, and especially, for the human mind, to bear . . . The pope, the Turks, the Jews, and all the sectarians (viz., the Anabaptists) pay no attention to this rule. They put Christ the mediator out of their sight, speak only of God, pray only to Him."[6] He also rejected the mystic's inward look: "[Repentance] simply lumps everything together and says, 'Everything is pure sin with us. What would we want to spend so much time investigating, dissecting, or distinguishing?'"[7] While still speaking of the importance

[4] AE, 26.34.

[5] E.g., his consistent rejection of the Anabaptist emphasis of having immediate revelations from God.

[6] AE, 26.28.

[7] "Smalcald Articles," in Robert Kolb and Timothy Wengert, eds., *The Book of Concord: The Confessions of the Evangelical Lutheran Church* (Minneapolis: Fortress Press, 2000), 318.

of godliness and the believer's union with Christ, Luther had moved from the mystic's focus on *Christus in nobis* to his later emphasis of *Christus pro nobis.*

Theses 1–12 of the disputation focused on the truth of the Law and works: They cannot help one come to know God. Reformation professor Timothy P. Dost has observed, "The Reformation was as much a recovery of the Law as it was a recovery of the gospel." Luther presented the Law in all its "unreasonable" perfection and majesty that people might flee to the gospel.[8] While continuing to think of the Law as God's *opus alienum*, Luther continued to sharpen his teaching on the Law to make an even crisper distinction between the Law and the gospel: "We should understand 'Law' to mean nothing else than God's word and command, in which He directs us what to do and what not to do, and demands from us our obedience and 'work.'"[9] He then defined the gospel: "On the other hand the Gospel or the faith is a doctrine or word of God that does not require our works. *It does not command us to do anything.* On the contrary, it bids us merely to accept the offered grace of forgiveness of sins and eternal life and let it be given to us."[10] While Luther continued to speak of God's alien work and His proper work, after Heidelberg the terms more often used to express these concepts were "Law" and "gospel."[11]

Theses 13–15 addressed the human will, the doctrine of which he did not change after Heidelberg. One may think of his 1525 work *On the Bondage of the Will*, an entire book that defends the same truth he taught at Heidelberg. Regarding the theology of the cross (theses 19–24), Luther continued to use this phrase throughout his career. Kolb observed that in July 1533, Luther lectured on Psalm 126,

---

[8] Timothy P. Dost, *The Reformation Era* (Christ College Irvine, CA, Spring 2015), and personal e-mail, January 29, 2018.

[9] Martin Luther, "The Distinction between the Law and Gospel," trans. Willard Burce, *January 1, 1532*, *Concordia Journal* 18 (April 1992): 156.

[10] Ibid., 157. Emphasis added.

[11] E.g., AE, 26.38: "The distinction between the 'proper work' of God and the 'alien work' of God . . . was basic to Luther's interpretation of the distinction between the Law and the Gospel" (Jaroslav Pelikan, footnote).

where the theology of the cross related to the believer's suffering. Yet Luther also possibly spoke of "God's revelation of his will through his Word."[12] Kolb concluded that the theology of the cross remained with Luther to the end and meant that (1) believers are to distinguish between the hidden and revealed God, (2) God has disclosed His essence by His sacrifice on the cross, (3) believers are to rely on faith in the Word over reason, (4) believers are to know how God acts by often hiding Himself in ways that seem contrary to His will and love, and (5) believers are to be encouraged as they battle, dying and rising in repentance.[13]

Theses 25–28 address righteousness, faith, and God's love. In these, we see the greatest change in Luther's teaching after Heidelberg. The following August after the disputation, Luther met Philip Melanchthon, who arrived in Wittenberg on August 25, 1518.[14] As previously stated, he was instrumental in helping Luther articulate his understanding of justification—viz., the doctrine of imputation and the definition of grace as a standing before God rather than a medicine. Imputation became his predominant way of believing in the atonement and the righteousness of God. Christ's active righteousness becomes the believer's passive righteousness.[15] "But this most excellent righteousness, the righteousness of faith, which God imputes to us through Christ without works . . . is a merely passive righteousness . . . For here we work nothing, render nothing to God; we only receive and permit someone else to work in us, namely, God."[16] Justification is forensic,[17] where imputation is added because of the weakness of faith.[18] While being forensic, jus-

---

[12] LTCF, 74. In this essay, Kolb also cites other works of Luther after Heidelberg.

[13] Ibid., 85.

[14] Philip Melanchthon, *Commonplaces: Loci Communes 1521*, ed. and trans. Christian Preus (St. Louis: Concordia, 2014), 5.

[15] Cf. "Two Kinds of Righteousness" (1519), AE, 31: 297–306.

[16] AE, 26: 4,5.

[17] Ibid., 109. "Our inherent holiness is not enough. Therefore Christ is our entire holiness; where this inherent holiness is not enough, Christ is."

[18] Cf. Luther on Galatians 3:6, ibid., 226–236.

tification is effective, making us practically righteous.[19] Faith in the disputation, while including trust, was mostly submission or humility before God. While Luther certainly considered humility to be important throughout his life, faith came to be more sharply defined as "trust"—that is, reliance on Christ and His atoning work being credited to one's account. Regarding thesis 28 on God's love, Luther did not change. Table 4.3 compares the Heidelberg Disputation with Luther's mature theology.

With this summary of the disputation in mind, it is fitting to return to the quote by Luther that opened this chapter: "For in my heart there rules this one doctrine, namely, faith in Christ. From it, through it, and to it all my theological thought flows and returns, day and night." Faith in Christ was the core of all Luther's theology, both at Heidelberg as well as in his later career. Faith in Christ was the wisdom of God that brought to nothing the wisdom of the world. In the

Table 4.3

The Heidelberg Disputation	Luther's Mature Theology
Faith is primarily defined as "humility/submission" to the wisdom and ways of God	Faith is defined as trust in the promises of God and in Christ's work on the cross
Grace is defined primarily as infused strength, yet alien	Grace is defined as an unmerited standing of favor before God
"The cross" is primarily suffering	"The cross" is suffering but also Christ's substitutionary atonement
"The Law" is the commandments of God	"The Law" is the commandments of God
Works cannot justify	Works cannot justify; Christ's alien righteousness alone is imputed to the sinner
Emphasis on *Christus* ***in*** *Nobis*	Emphasis on *Christus* ***pro*** *Nobis*
Emphasis on God's subjective work	Emphasis on God's objective work in Christ
"Opus alienum" and *"opus proprium"*	*"The Law and the Gospel"* is used to express the truths of *"opus alienum"* and *"opus proprium"*

[19] Ibid.

final analysis, the Heidelberg Disputation was the embryonic form of Protestant doctrine that comforted—yet disturbed—the world.

Summary

While the disputation was a very early form of Luther's understanding of the message of the cross, it proved to be a paradigm for his mature theology. He retained all the categories of the disputation throughout his career. His teaching on works, grace, human will, and justification fell as a hammer on the European Church while at the same time creating a framework for Protestant theology.

As this study comes to an end, there is still work to be done. As Dennis Bielfeldt noted, Harold Grimm's translation of the philosophical theses was well-meaning yet done before the philosophical proofs were published.[20] A more accurate translation of the theses and the proofs needs to be rendered along with more thorough commentary that is based on a great grasp of philosophy. Second, work can be done using the Heidelberg Disputation as an apologetic for sharing the Christian message with the world. For this document so succinctly "calls the thing what it actually is,"[21] thereby exposing the faulty scaffolding and ideological foundations of all civilization.[22] True guilt before a holy God can thus be once again known to a world that declares itself innocent. With the owning of guilt, perhaps the West will once again know grace that is found only at the foot of the cross.

Study of the disputation has produced some surprising results. First, studying it in its original context, one sees that the work is not as "Protestant" as it first appears, though it certainly is a beautiful outline of the gospel message. Along with this, one is surprised to note that Luther's understanding of the gospel did not come all at

---

[20] PT, 4.

[21] HD, thesis 21.

[22] This is not to deny the legitimacy of God's left-hand kingdom, which He has raised up for the benefit of all (e.g., cf. Rom. 13:1–7). Rather, the disputation does reveal the sinful nature of us all and thus our trust in ourselves, which brings destruction on ourselves and society.

once but over a period of years. This is heartening, for none of us grasps the gospel as we should. Even in 1535, Luther saw his continual need to grow in understanding the riches of the gospel. We should be patient with ourselves and others who come out of a lifetime of works-religion.

There is a third surprise. One is struck by how the outline of the disputation—that is, its theology—lays flat the children of pride throughout the earth, for it places rich and poor, godly and godless, strong and weak on the same level. It is an awe-inspiring fact that God cannot be known by human wisdom (i.e., by our own works or human reason) but can only be known in suffering and the cross (i.e., by being led to the end of ourselves to the foot of Him who had no majesty and died helpless on the cross for us [Isa. 53:2, 6]). No one has anything to give God. We only have our crucified Savior who became nothing that He might meet us in our sin and weakness: "For since in the wisdom of God the world through its wisdom did not come to know God, God was well-pleased through the foolishness of the message preached to save those who believe" (1 Cor. 1:21).

Afterword

In the sixteenth century, society experienced upheaval as a result of the theology of the Heidelberg Disputation being proclaimed and embraced by the Protestant reformers. Five hundred years later, the West is once again in upheaval as the truths of the Heidelberg Disputation are being *rejected*. The losses have been incalculable.

John Morley was an admirer of the 1700's Enlightenment and its effect upon Western civilization. In Morley's estimation, "The Goddess of Reason" had been enthroned,[1] and through the work of Voltaire, Rousseau, Diderot, and his *Encyclopedia*, the scaffolding was assembled for the building of a thoroughly secularized Europe. Summarizing the central pillar of Enlightenment thought, Morley wrote, "that human nature is good. . . . This cheerful doctrine now strikes on the ear as a commonplace and a truism. A hundred years ago in France, it was a wonderful gospel, and the beginning of a new dispensation."[2] Owen Chadwick concisely summarized Morley's observation and its effect: "Human nature is good. This, said Morley, is the key that secularizes the world."[3]

The Enlightenment's rejection of the Heidelberg Disputation's anthropology has continued to this day, causing a serious erosion to all categories of Christian theology. After all, if man can save himself,

---

[1] John Morley, *Diderot and the Encyclopaedists*, volume 1 (London: Chapman and Hall, 1873), 2.

[2] Ibid., 5.

[3] Owen Chadwick, *The Secularization of the European Mind in the Nineteenth Century* (Cambridge: Cambridge University Press, 1975, 1990), 152. I am indebted to C. FitzSimons Allison for the discovery of Chadwick's work.

what need is there for the cross or the gospel? We can somehow stand before the God of Isaiah dressed in a wedding garment of our own making and thus compromise His holiness. While the disputation declared Gabriel Biel's semi-Pelagianism to be as an unclean leper, both Western civilization and even the Church have warmly welcomed the leper back into the camp. To borrow Morley's phrase, we in the twenty-first century are calling semi-Pelagianism a "wonderful gospel." The result is that we have lost the *gravitas* of God, we have minimized the atonement and forensic justification, we have lost our sense of need for the gospel of grace. We have antiphonally answered the angels' praise that broke Bethlehem's night with a dissonant chorus of our own making: "Glory to Man in the Highest."

In short, through our high view of human nature, we have become theologians of glory.

On a cold December morning, my wife and I drove by live oak trees in South Carolina's Low Country to visit C. FitzSimons and Martha Allison. They so kindly opened their home and hearts to us—a newly married couple whom they had never met. At their entryway was a curious sight: a plumb line hung from the balcony. We later discovered the purpose of the plumb line: referring to the book of Amos, it was to be a reminder to Bishop Allison of the unflinching and unchanging perfection of the Law of God. Whenever he would lift up his heart in pride or begin to think that somehow he had gone beyond his need for the cross, there hung the plumb line, silently reminding him of the truth of his own heart. He would be driven back to Christ.

My friend's plumb line was Luther's plumb line—the pure and holy Law of God, thundering from heaven to a world lifted up in pride. Five hundred years of ideological change has not altered the inviolable Law of God—though we have tried with all our might to erase transcendent truth from the world. Plumb lines don't lie. They only tell the truth; the plumb line of the Law tells us the truth about human nature and exposes our guilt.

As John Newton (the author of *Amazing Grace*) observed, "Guilt is the parent of atheism." We may try to alleviate our guilt before the Law of God by ridding the universe of God's existence, or by ridding God of His thunder and thus making Him like us, or by passing laws to justify our sin, or by hiding in our semi-Pelagian castles, defending ourselves, as Luther said, by exalting "free will." In any of these solutions, we become our own arbiter of truth, seeking a dynasty change in heaven.

There is another possible response we may have to our guilt—a response to which the Heidelberg Disputation kindly invites us. With nothing in our hands but sin, we may humbly admit our spiritual poverty before the Law of God and trust in the finished work of Christ for us, resting from our own works. Such trust will come face-to-face with the meekness of the Lamb of God, in whom alone we find rest. Such trust will restore health to the life of the Church and once again give us a clear message to share with the world. As a friend of mine observed, one who is genuinely poor in spirit will never add to the gospel; rather, he or she will embrace the word of the cross and proclaim it with clarity and simplicity.

While the Enlightenment architects drew plans for a magisterial throne for the kingdom of reason, another man from the eighteenth century—the poet William Cowper—was given the ability to see the truth of man's so-called righteousness and the truth of God's sweet grace. He called "the thing what it actually is," to use Luther's phrase, seeing both the hideousness of our self-righteousness and the beautiful and simple truth of Christ's promise and saving work. Describing the thief who was crucified along with Christ on Good Friday afternoon, Cowper wrote,

> The dying thief rejoic'd to see that fountain in his day,
> and there have I, as vile as he, wash'd all my sins away.

In describing the thief, Cowper also described himself. May we, like the thief on the cross, like William Cowper, and like Martin Luther, embrace the truths in the Heidelberg Disputation and know God only in the cross of Christ. May we believers in Christ ever remain there and thus flee the plague of the theology of glory. And as the apostle Paul expressed in his letter to the Corinthians, may we ever determine to know nothing before the world save the word of the cross: Jesus Christ and Him crucified.

Appendix

Martin Bucer's Letter to Beatus Rhenanus

Martin Bucer (1491–1551) was present at the disputation. He would later become a major leader in the Reformation and would have much influence in Strasbourg and on John Calvin as well as Thomas Cranmer and the Reformation movement in England. A few days after the disputation ended, Bucer wrote a letter on May 1 to Beatus Rhenanus (a friend and assistant to Erasmus who lived in Basle in 1518), describing the disputation's setting, Luther's demeanor, and how the disputation was received. The letter also gives a sense of the religious world in 1518. Bucer wrote this letter as an Erasmian who did not yet consider himself to be among Luther's number. However, he applauded Luther and spoke of his consistency with Erasmus as well as his more open and free teaching of Erasmus's work. Along with Luther, Bucer condemned Aristotle and his influence on the church. This letter also gave an account of Bucer's personal interview with Luther the following day.

"Martin Bucer to Beatus Rhenanus at Basle"[1]

"I have read your attack on our theologians, and I should have been sorry had it been vain. Wherefore, lest you should seem to yourself to have triumphed, after we Heidelbergers had deserted the cause (for it fared otherwise with our elder Wimpfeling, although he defended us nobly), I will oppose to you a certain theologian, not, indeed, one

[1] Martin Bucer, "Martin Bucer to Beatus Rhenanus at Basle," in Preserved Smith, trans. and ed., *Luther's Correspondence and Other Contemporary Letters, Vol. 1, 1507–1521* (Philadelphia: Lutheran Publication Society, 1913), 80–83.

of our number, but one who has been heard by us in the last few days, one who has got so far away from the bonds of the sophists and the trifling of Aristotle, one who is so devoted to the Bible, and is so suspicious of antiquated theologians of our school (for their eloquence forces us to call them theologians and rhetoricians, too), that he appears to be diametrically opposed to our teachers. Jerome, Augustine and the authors of that stamp are as familiar to him as Scotus or Tartaretus could be to us. He is Martin Luther, that abuser of indulgences, on which we have hitherto relied too much. At the general chapter of his order celebrated here, according to the custom, he presided over a debate, and propounded some paradoxes, which not only went farther than most could follow him, but appeared to some heretical. But, good Heavens! what real authentic theologian would these men approve, whose touchstone in approving or condemning doctrines is Aristotle, or rather the pestilent poison disseminated by his corrupters? Why should I not say this frankly of the foolish trifling with which they drench and foul the divine food of our minds, the holy oracles and their most holy interpreters, and thus make men forget the noble artificer of celestial splendor? But I repress my most just wrath against them lest they should make too much of sportive beginnings.

To return to Martin Luther: although our chief men refuted him with all their might, their wiles were not able to make him move an inch from his propositions. His sweetness in answering is remarkable, his patience in listening is incomparable, in his explanations you would recognize the acumen of Paul, not of Scotus; his answers, so brief, so wise, and drawn from the Holy Scriptures, easily made all his hearers his admirers.

On the next day I had a familiar and friendly conference with the man alone, and a supper rich with doctrine rather than with dainties. He lucidly explained whatever I might ask. He agrees with Erasmus in all things, but with this difference in his favor, that what Erasmus only insinuates he teaches openly and freely. Would that I had time to write you more of this. He has brought it about that at Wittenberg the ordinary textbooks have all been abolished, while the Greeks, and Jerome, Augustine and Paul are publicly taught.

But you see there is no room to write more. I enclose his paradoxes and their explanations, as far as I was able to take them down during the disputation or was taught them by him afterwards. I expect you will be much pleased to see them; if not, take them in the spirit in which they were sent. . . .

(Among the theses from the Heidelberg Disputation enclosed by Bucer are the following:[2])

I. The law of God, that most wholesome instruction unto life, is not able to justify a man, but rather hinders this.

III. It is probable that the works of men which seem to be specious and good are really mortal sins.

XIII. Since the fall, free will is a mere name; when the will does what is in its power it sins mortally."

[2] Editor's comment in the original.

Glossary

alien and proper righteousness. *Alien* righteousness is righteousness that is bestowed from outside of a person. It is freely given by sheer grace, apart from any work within a person. This is distinguished from *proper* righteousness—actual and ethical righteousness performed by a person.[1]

christus in nobis. "Christ in us." In Luther's early years, he emphasized Christ's work in a believer—viz., the believer's union with Christ. As his theology developed, he would come to emphasize Christ for us (*Christus pro nobis*)—viz., His keeping the Law for us, His dying on the cross for us, His rising from the dead for us.

christus pro nobis. "Christ for us." (See also previous definition of *Christus in nobis.*)

cross. In Luther's early years, "the cross" pertained more to God's alien work of suffering and humbling the sinner. The cross also referred to God being manifested in Christ's suffering and death and was associated with Luther's "theology of humility" (cf. following definition). While Luther retained these concepts in varying degrees, the cross would later come to refer to Christ's substitutionary atonement for sinners: Christ taking the curse and the wrath of the Law upon Himself that believers may be freely justified. At Heidelberg, Luther's understanding of the atonement was both subjective and

---

[1] OX, 639, 647.

objective: subjective like Abelard's doctrine of the atonement, objective like Anselm's doctrine.[2]

crux sola est nostra theologia. "The cross alone is our theology." This sentence is found in Luther's 1519 lectures on the Psalms. In this, he meant that human suffering and conviction of guilt denote "the cross." This leads the sinner to a true understanding of all categories of theology where one sees clearly who Christ is and an entire trust in Him as a result of being humbled.

deus absconditus / revelatus. "Luther's distinguished 'God hidden' . . . and 'God revealed' . . . Luther also taught that the revealed God hides himself in crib and cross, by taking form in humble ways that human reason finds unworthy of the Divine."[3] This distinction in Luther's theology remained at the heart of the Heidelberg Disputation and his doctrine of God throughout his career. The unpreached God is *Deus absconditus:* God hidden. The God who is preached from the Word and the promise of the gospel is *Deus revelatus:* God revealed.

disputation. "A form of instruction and testing in the medieval university, begun in Western schools, building on an ancient tradition, in the twelfth and thirteenth centuries. Disputations were formal argumentative exchanges designed to assess students' abilities in logic and rhetoric or to give instructors the field on which to discuss their ideas and exchange points of view."[4]

faith. In his early years, Luther defined faith as submission or humility—that is, letting God be God, accepting His ways and trusting Him. In later years, Luther sharpened his understanding of faith to mean trust or reliance upon the person and work of Christ to freely justify sinners.

free will. A concept found in medieval theology, where the human will is free to choose God and godliness of its own volition. Luther

[2] Cf. Ibid., 158.

[3] Ibid., 641.

[4] OX, 641.

said that this was not true; rather, free will is, after the fall, "in name only." Only in decisions not related to God, such as choosing what color shirt to wear, did Luther say the will was free. He retained this understanding of the human will to the end of his life.

grace. In his early years, as well as at Heidelberg, Luther considered grace to be defined as strength that was infused into a person, enabling one to produce fruit. Shortly after Heidelberg, Melanchthon showed Luther that grace meant favor, a standing with God not based on merit. Erasmus agreed with Melanchthon's definition of grace.

iustitia. Righteousness—viz., a righteous standing with God freely given through faith alone.

justification. Luther described justification as "'through faith' . . . we receive a different, new, clean heart and that, for the sake of Christ our mediator, God will and does regard us as completely righteous and holy. Although sin in the flesh is still not completely gone or dead, God will nevertheless not count or consider it."[5] Mark Mattes observes that Luther understood justification to be both forensic (a declaration of being accounted righteous) *and* effective (resulting in an actual righteous conduct that springs from being forensically justified).[6] Luther's forensic view of justification was not fully developed until after Heidelberg. However, the disputation's main argument seems to contain an embryonic form of forensic justification.

law. Luther's use of the word "Law" in the disputation meant every law of God—specifically, the Ten Commandments. This definition differed from Jerome and Erasmus, who considered Paul's use of the Law to be only the ceremonial law (cf. previous exposition of thesis one in chapter 3).

mysticism. A movement in the medieval church that sought to know God by immediate knowledge apart from justification and atonement (cf. chapter 2, "Mysticism").

---

[5] Ibid., 264.

[6] Ibid., 265.

opus alienum. God's "alien or strange work"—that is, God's work of humbling a sinner through suffering and conviction of sin to cause the sinner to look outside of himself to Christ alone for salvation. In this work, God appears to human reason as hateful and cruel. It is a work that is outside the nature of God, according to Luther.

opus proprium. God's "proper work," whereby He brings a person to trust in Christ alone for salvation, thus justifying the sinner. God's alien work (see aforementioned *opus alienum*) leads to God's proper work. God's alien and proper works are discussed in theses 16–18 of the disputation.

scholasticism. "A particular approach to Christian theology, associated especially with the Middle Ages, which lays emphasis upon the rational justification and systematic presentation of Christian theology."[7] Especially in his early career, Luther wrote against scholasticism, claiming that its stress on reason, among other issues, eroded the gospel message.

simul iustus et peccator. "At the same time justified and sinner." This was an important part of Luther's understanding of the nature of a Christian. He used this phrase even in the early years of his career, showing that a true child of God is declared righteous before God—even while remaining sinful.

sin, mortal. (*peccata mortalia*) Sin that damns a person to hell and remains unforgiven.

sin, venial. (*peccata venialia*) Sins that are mere weaknesses and do not damn to hell.

theology of glory. (*theologia gloriae*) "Luther's term for the rationalistic theology of the scholastics that discussed God in terms of his glorious attributes rather than in terms of his self-revelation in suffering and cross."[8]

---

[7] Alister McGrath, *Historical Theology: An Introduction to the History of Christian Thought* (Oxford: Blackwell, 1998), 353.

[8] Ibid., 302.

theology of humility. Luther's early theology in which one humbly came to the end of himself, judged himself as guilty before God, and "let God be God," accepting who He is and His ways. This was influenced by Luther's early exposure to mysticism and is woven into the Heidelberg Disputation. While he kept aspects of the theology of humility throughout his career, his mature theology focused more on Christ *for* us—that is, His objective work on the cross and justification by faith alone—and not as much on Christ's work *in* us for justification.

theology of the cross. (*theologia crucis*) "A term used by Luther and is descriptive of his insight into the nature of revelation and therefore of theology as a whole. God has chosen to reveal himself, not as human reason has chosen to describe him in its rational theology of glory (*theologia gloriae*), but in the weakness and scandal of the cross."[9]

---

[9] Richard A. Muller, *Dictionary of Latin and Greek Theological Terms* (Grand Rapids: Baker Academic, 1985, 1995), 300.

Select Bibliography

Aristotle. *The Nicomachean Ethics*. Translated by David Ross. Oxford: Oxford University Press, 2009.

Augustine. "On the Spirit and the Letter." In *The Nicene and Post-Nicene Fathers, Vol. 5*, edited by Philip Schaff, 79–114. Grand Rapids: Eerdmans, 1971.

Bagchi, David, and David C. Steinmetz, eds. *The Cambridge Companion to Reformation Theology*. Cambridge: Cambridge University Press, 2004.

Barzun, Jacques. *From Dawn to Decadence: 500 Years of Western Cultural Life*. New York: HarperCollins, 2000.

Batka, L'ubomír, Irene Dingel, and Robert Kolb, eds. *The Oxford Handbook of Martin Luther's Theology*. Oxford: Oxford University Press, 2014.

Bielfeldt, Dennis. *The Philosophical Theses and Demonstrations of the Heidelberg Disputation*. Institute of Lutheran Theology, October 2015.

Brecht, Martin. *Martin Luther: His Road to Reformation 1483–1521*. Philadelphia: Fortress Press, 1985.

Brown, Colin. *Christianity and Western Thought: Volume 1: From the Ancient World to the Age of Enlightenment*. Downers Grove: InterVarsity Press, 1990.

Cameron, Euan. *The European Reformation*. Oxford: Oxford University Press, 1991, 2012.

Clark, Kelly James, Richard Lints, and James K. A. Smith. *101 Key Terms in Philosophy and Their Importance for Theology*. Louisville: Westminster John Knox Press, 2004.

Eire, Carlos M. N. *Reformations: The Early Modern World, 1450–1650*. New Haven: Yale University Press, 2016.

Forde, Gerhard O. *On Being a Theologian of the Cross: Reflections on Luther's Heidelberg Disputation, 1518*. Grand Rapids: Eerdmans, 1997.

Godfrey, W. Robert. *Reformation Sketches*. Phillipsburg: P&R Publishing, 2003.

Green, Lowell. *How Melanchthon Helped Luther Discover the Gospel: The Doctrine of Justification in the Reformation*. Fallbrook: Verdict Publications, 1980.

Hendrix, Scott H. *Martin Luther: Visionary Reformer*. New Haven: Yale University Press, 2015.

Keith, Scott L. "Creeds and Confessions." Christ College Irvine, Summer 2016.

Kittelson, James M. *Luther the Reformer: The Story of the Man and His Career*. Minneapolis: Fortress Press, 1986.

Kolb, Robert. "Luther on the Theology of the Cross." *Lutheran Quarterly* 16 (2002): 443–466.

———. "Luther's Theology of the Cross Fifteen Years after Heidelberg: Lectures on the Psalms of Ascent." *Journal of Ecclesiastical History* 61, no. 1 (January 2010): 69–85.

Kolb, Robert, and Timothy J. Wengert, eds. *The Book of Concord: The Confessions of the Evangelical Lutheran Church*. Minneapolis: Fortress Press, 2000.

Lindberg, Carter, ed. *The European Reformations Sourcebook*. Oxford: Wiley and Sons, 2014.

Lockwood, Gregory J. *1 Corinthians*. St. Louis: Concordia, 2000.

Loewenich, Walther von. *Luther's Theology of the Cross*. Translated by Herbert J. A. Bouman. Minneapolis: Augsburg, 1976.

Luther, Martin. *The Bondage of the Will*. Translated by J. I. Packer and O. R. Johnston. Grand Rapids: Baker Academic, 1957, 2012.

———. "The Distinction between the Law and the Gospel." Translated by Willard Burce. *Concordia Journal* 18 (April 1992): 153–163.

———. "The Heidelberg Disputation." In *The Annotated Luther, Volume 1: The Roots of Reform*, edited by Timothy J. Wengert, 80–88. Minneapolis: Fortress Press, 2015.

———. *Luther's Works 1–55*, edited by H. Lehman, J. Pelikan, et al. St. Louis: Concordia, 1955–1986.

———. "Probationes Conclusionum: Quae in Capitulo Heidelbergensi Disputatae Sunt." In *(Weimar Ausgabe) D. Martin Luthers Werke: Kritische Gesamtausgabe* 1, edited by H. Bölau, 355–374. Germany: Verlag Hermann Böhlaus Nachfolger Weimar, 2003.

———. "Proofs of the Thesis Debated in the Chapter of Heidelberg, May, AD 1518." In *The Annotated Luther, Volume 1: The Roots of Reform*, edited by Timothy J. Wengert, 80–120. Minneapolis: Fortress Press, 2015.

MacCulloch, Diarmaid. *All Things Made New: The Reformation and Its Legacy*. Oxford: Oxford University Press, 2016.

Mallinson, Jeff. "Christianity, Ethics, and Contemporary Culture." Christ College Irvine, Fall 2015.

McGrath, Alister E. *Historical Theology: An Introduction to the History of Christian Thought*. Oxford: Blackwell, 1998.

———. *Luther's Theology of the Cross: Martin Luther's Theological Breakthrough*. Oxford: Blackwell, 1985.

Melanchthon, Philip. *Commonplaces: Loci Communes 1521*. Edited and translated by Christian Preus. St. Louis: Concordia, 2014.

Muller, Richard A. *Dictionary of Latin and Greek Theological Terms*. Grand Rapids: Baker Academic, 1985, 1995.

New American Standard Bible. La Habra: The Lockman Foundation, 1960, 1995.

Ozment, Steven. *The Age of Reform, 1250–1550: An Intellectual and Religious History of Late Medieval and Reformation Europe*. New Haven: Yale University Press, 1980.

Pettegree, Andrew, ed. *The Reformation World*. London: Routledge, 2000.

Smith, Preserved, ed. and trans. *Luther's Correspondence and Other Contemporary Letters, Vol. 1: 1507–1521*. Philadelphia: Lutheran Publication Society, 1913.

Spitz, Lewis W. *The Renaissance and Reformation Movements, Volume 1*. St. Louis: Concordia, 1971, 1987.

Thiselton, Anthony C. *NIGTC: The First Epistle to the Corinthians*. Grand Rapids: Eerdmans, 2000.

Vercruysse, Joseph E. "Luther's Theology of the Cross at the Time of the Heidelberg Disputation." *Gregorianum* 57, no. 3 (1976): 523–548.

Walther, C. F. W. *The Proper Distinction between Law and Gospel*. St. Louis: Concordia, 1929, 1986.

Wengert, Timothy J., ed. *The Annotated Luther, Volume 1: The Roots of Reform*. Minneapolis: Fortress Press, 2015.

Wright, William J. *Martin Luther's Understanding of God's Two Kingdoms: A Response to the Challenge of Skepticism*. Grand Rapids: Baker Academic, 2010.

Made in the USA
Las Vegas, NV
21 December 2021